Getting the Buggers to Find Out

Information Skills and Learning How to Learn

DUNCAN GREY

D0452963

continuum

Continuum International Publishing Group
The Tower Building   80 Maiden Lane
11 York Road   Suite 704
London   New York
SE1 7NX   NY 10038

www.continuumbooks.com

British Library Cataloguing-in-Publication Data
A catalogue record for this book is available from the British Library.

ISBN: 9–7808–2649–9738 (paperback/hardcover)

Library of Congress Cataloging-in-Publication Data
Grey, Duncan.
   Getting the buggers to find out / Duncan Grey.
      p. cm.
   Includes bibliographical references and index.
   ISBN 978-0-8264-9973-8
   1. Information literacy–Study and teaching. 2. Information resources–Evaluation–Study and teaching. 3. Computer network resources–Evaluation–Study and teaching. 4. Information retrieval--Study and teaching. 5. Teachers–In-service training.   I. Title.

   ZA3075.G74.2008
   028.7071–dc22

2008008270

Typeset by BookEns Ltd, Royston, Herts.
Printed and bound in Great Britain by Cromwell Press Ltd, Wiltshire.

Contents

Acknowledgements   ix
Preface   xi
Introduction   1

1   Why is information literacy important?   9
    Core knowledge   11
    Reliability   12
    Shelf guides for the global library   14
    The knowledge economy   15
    Comparing sources   16
    Different views   21

2   Information literacy across the curriculum   23
    The information literacy strand   23
    National Curriculum and examples   25
    Successful learners   31
    Functional skills   32
    Key processes   32
    Literacy strategy   41
    Curriculum activities using information literacy   44

3   The 20 main skills of information literacy   54
    Questions   57
    Defining the task   60
    Making decisions   62
    Brainstorming   64
    Problem solving   65
    Identifying sources   67
    Locating sources   68

Selecting sources		70
Finding information within sources		71
Reading for meaning		72
Skimming and scanning		74
Evaluating material		76
Note-making		79
Sorting and arranging		81
Developing ideas		82
Presenting findings		84
Writing clearly		88
Rhetoric		90
Citing sources		93
Evaluation and review		96
4	**Methodical strategies**	**99**
	Case studies	99
	Accepted models	104
	Advantages and disadvantages	107
	Three new models	108
	Conclusion	110
5	**Practical strategies for implementation in your school**	**115**
	SWOT analysis	115
	Persuasion	116
	Bribery	117
	Working parties and committees	118
	Timetabling	119
	Policies	120
	Personality	120
	Action plan	121
	An information audit	123
	Information privacy	127
	Cyberbullying	129
	Information security	129
	Limiting risk	130
	Identity theft	131
	Plagiarism	133

Garbled information 135
Backups 136
Putting it all together 137
Information skills strategy 137
What do I do now? 138

6 Using your Resources Centre and your librarian 141
The Resources Centre 141
The librarian 142
Building blocks for library success 142
Learning in the library without walls 143
Roles and responsibilities 143
Librarians can help 144
Teachers can help 145
Why create more resources? 145
Use the Learning Resources Centre 146
More information 147
A sample library/resources policy 148

7 Search engines and computer skills 153
Search engines 153
Search words 155
Improving your searches in Google 155
Library catalogues 158
Processing 159
Other ICT tools 159
Desktop features 160
Web browsers and extensions 160
RSS 161
Email tools 161
Personal home/start pages 162
Search and research tools 162
Text processors 162
Organizers 163
Presentations 164
The future 166

8   Taking part in the global conversation   169
Wikis, blogs and personal websites   170
Information systems   170
Limitless information   172
Document management   175
Content management   176
Semantic web   176
The future of information   177

Further reading   180

Appendix 1   Information literacy and the National   186
              Literacy Strategy
Appendix 2   Questions and decisions 1   190
Appendix 3   Questions and decisions 2   191
Appendix 4   Define the task   192
Appendix 5   Problem solving: the SWOT analysis   194
Appendix 6   Identifying sources   196
Appendix 7   Selecting sources   198
Appendix 8   Evaluating material   200
Appendix 9   The argument table   202
Appendix 10   Evaluation   204
Appendix 11   Which model suits us best?   208

Index   209

Acknowledgements

I am grateful for the help of those people who described to me their methods of using information: Dr John Coppendale, Dr Sarah Coppendale, Dr John Doviak, Catherine Grey, Dr Hugh Pelham. Although I have edited what they said I have tried not to misrepresent them.

I should like to thank the many school librarians I have met over the years, especially those who have attended my information skills courses. I am particularly grateful to Sue Hyde, a colleague, a very practical librarian and voice of reason for many years.

Some of the material in this book was first published in 2006 as *Implementing an Information Literacy Programme in Your School*.

Preface

This book is about 'finding out'. Is there any one of us who does not need to find out?

This book aims to help you to find out more conveniently and more accurately. It offers suggestions of how to build up a toolkit of skills we can all take with us to use when our 'one small head' is not enough, when our encyclopedia is not at hand and our remembered knowledge does not stretch far enough. If you are a teacher, it also aims to help you to give your pupils a set of finding-out tools that will last a lifetime.

An ever-expanding quantity of data surrounds us, and if we are to make any sense of it we need to ask the right questions, discriminate between useful and unhelpful data, select and verify what we need and discard what is superfluous or incorrect, synthesize information from different sources, present our findings in a useful way and evaluate what we have done.

This is how we can find answers in a reasonable time, answer reasonable questions with a fair degree of accuracy, update and revise our existing knowledge, examine and review new information and expand and develop our understanding in an ever-changing world. 'How to find out' is the skill that enables learning for life.

Information can be used positively to inform and enhance understanding, but it can also be used to reduce individuality to a column of numbers. A methodical approach to information *enables* creativity, it should not crush it. Whether you are with the bean counters or The Prisoner:

> I will not be pushed, filed, stamped, indexed, briefed, debriefed or numbered. My life is my own.
>
> (*The Prisoner* 1967)

the skills of making sense of information in an information-rich world are vital.

This book doesn't give you the answers – it gives you the tools to ask and to answer the questions yourself. That way you are in a position to find the answer to *every* question.

Duncan Grey
Cambridge, May 2008

'Where am I?'
'In the Village.'
'What do you want?'
'Information.'
'Whose side are you on?'
'That would be telling ... We want information.
Information! INFORMATION!'

The Prisoner 1967

INTRODUCTION

Introduction

What is information literacy?

> Information Literacy is the ability to locate pertinent information, evaluate its reliability, analyse and synthesise the information to construct personal meaning and apply it to informed decision making.
>
> (Berger 1998)

Or to put it another way, 'information literacy' is the skill of finding out. Because 'finding out' can seem a complex process I've identified a series of stages or steps to go through methodically – a well-trodden finding-out route we can all follow, whatever the task or the question. This route has many junctions and side roads which I'll signpost along the way, but the main route is vitally important even where it isn't clear and obvious.

Apart from courses and formal education, most of us find things out in a random and disorganized way. It's one of the joys of learning, to chance upon something and feel you've discovered it for yourself. There's even a word for it: 'serendipity' – the accidental discovery of something fortunate while looking for something else entirely.

There are many examples of scientists discovering one thing while either looking for something else (Uranus the planet found while looking for a comet; bioelectricity found while dissecting a frog; mauve dye found while trying to create artificial quinine; Scotchguard moisture repellant found when material spilled on the scientist's tennis shoes; Teflon found while searching for a new refrigeration gas). However it's important to make the point that the mind of the scientist has to be open and able first to recognize then apply the knowledge.

If Fleming had not been curious about the mould in his dish and how the bacteria had been killed, then applied his extensive research into antibacterial substances, we would not have had penicillin; if the Canon engineer who accidentally put his hot soldering iron on his pen had not noticed that ink was suddenly ejected from the pen's point, or had not thought about the implications of the event, the principle behind inkjet printers would not have been found.

2

Many other discoveries are made less by chance than by methodical questioning. Strategies range from repeatedly asking 'why' to using a series of questions planned according to previous knowledge.

Why is the sky blue?
Because on a clear day molecules in the air scatter blue light from the sun more than they scatter red light.
But why is it red at the end of the day?
Because sunlight passes a longer distance through air and some of the blue light has been scattered away. If the air is polluted with small particles, the sunset will be more red.
Why?
Because of the Rayleigh effect: the amount of light scattered is inversely proportional to the fourth power of wavelength for sufficiently small particles.
    Oh . . ..

Or

Where did you go that night?
I went home.
How did you get there?
By bus.
Which bus?
The 37.
And where did you get off?
At Weidner Road.
At what time?
10.05.
Precisely?
I think so.
How do you know?
I checked on my watch.
Why? Show me your watch, who saw you arrive?
Etc.

Often we ask a question and make do with an unconfirmed or imprecise answer. By asking a vague question, we tend to receive a vague and unverified answer, then accept it in a vague and half-satisfied way.

Here are two examples.

> **A.**
> I have two wall clocks in my kitchen. Over breakfast I look at the old mechanical clock and see it's time to go. I then glance at the battery-operated clock on the other wall to confirm that the time is accurate. If they are different, perhaps because the mechanical clock needs winding, I have to make a decision about the exact time. I could check my wristwatch as a third source but I rarely do, I just accept a rough approximation and leave home, in what I hope is in time for work.

What do I learn from this? On the one hand, if I'm prepared to accept this approximation with something as definite as time measurement, what am I prepared to tolerate with less clear facts? On the other hand, I have at least tried to find confirming evidence from more than one source.

> **B.**
> Catherine: Dad, where's Iraq?
> Dad: Oh, it's over in the Middle East, near Iran.
> Catherine: So is that near Turkey?
> Dad: Mmm ... kind of ...

If that reminds you of a typical exchange, think about what this means for the education of our children. What lessons can we learn from it?

1. *What do we really want to know?*
   Although it seems a straightforward question, we don't know if there is a deeper question underlying it. Is the purpose to place Iraq on a globe, to relate its position to other

countries in the Middle East, to start exploring its significance in political affairs or any one of a hundred other possibilities? Dad has missed the chance to develop the interest and Catherine is unsatisfied.

2. *Teaching the art of questioning*

    A lesson from this is that we must teach the art of questioning. Is the first question we ask the only question? Is it a question designed to get the answer we want? An imprecise quiz question will annoy the audience if it is too vague, can be answered in several different ways or has several different possible answers. Without a known context, 'What's the high jump record?' has a different answer depending on whether the subject is male or female, from a particular age group, a particular country or region, human or a grasshopper.

3. *Using the best resources*

    Dad evidently doesn't know the answer to this question, but avoids admitting it. Was he the best source of knowledge? Either he or Catherine could have used an atlas for a more accurate answer. If Dad had helped Catherine to use an atlas she might have been better prepared the next time she had a similar question. On the other hand, spending too long finding an accurate answer might have switched Catherine off when she could have been satisfied with a simple answer. In which case back to point 1 above.

4. *Asking the right question*

    This is the first step in a complex series of steps towards finding out. Sometimes the question is wrapped in a task given by a teacher to pupils. Defining the task is every bit as important as asking the right question. At all costs avoid saying, 'Find out everything you can about ...'. I hope this book is the antidote to that kind of unachievable task set too often by teachers with an unclear idea of what they want pupils to learn.

Asking the right question can mean looking closely at the assumptions we make.

Introduction

> Dad: ... and people in China use chopsticks instead of knives and forks.
> Catherine (aged 4):   So how do they spread marmalade on their toast?

And it's not just children who start with false assumptions.

> Caller to computer help desk: The wire on the mouse is too short! What can I do?
> Help desk: Too short? How is it too short?
> Caller: I'm trying to move the arrow on the screen but I can't pull the mouse any further down. I've run out of table!
> Help desk: Try lifting the mouse up and putting it back on the mouse mat ....

Another example relates to our environment. There is a commonly held belief that supermarket plastic bags cause death in birds, dolphins and turtles. The claim is that plastic bags kill 100,000 animals and 1,000,000 birds every year and UK Government policy was influenced by this.

However *The Times* (8 March 2008) established that 'there is no scientific evidence to show that the bags pose any direct threat to marine mammals'. *The Times* said the claim was based on a misinterpretation of a 1987 Canadian study, misquoted in a 2002 Australian report and 'latched on to by conservationists as proof that the bags were killers'. The typo remained uncorrected for four years, when 'plastic bags' was replaced by 'plastic debris'. Bias and error combine to create ill-conceived policy.

Alvin Toffler said:

> The illiterate of the future will not be those who cannot read and write, but those who cannot learn, unlearn, and relearn.
> (Toffler 1970)

Information literacy is a set of skills which enable people to learn, unlearn and relearn. These skills enable lifelong learning, to compensate for what we failed to learn at school, to give us knowledge of a new field if we change careers, to teach us about new developments unheard of while we were in full-time education and to get us through our lives.

Where teachers once simply 'filled little heads with knowledge', I suggest we might want to see ourselves more broadly as educators, encouraging the learning of fundamental skills and guiding pupils towards *finding out for themselves.*

The main skills

I have identified 20 main skills, which together make up information literacy. These are:

> Questions; Defining the task; Making decisions; Brainstorming; Problem solving; Identifying sources; Locating sources; Selecting sources; Finding information within sources; Reading for meaning; Skimming and scanning; Evaluating material; Note-making; Sorting and arranging; Developing ideas; Presenting findings; Writing clearly; Rhetoric; Citing sources; Evaluation and review.

These are all important components, and many are already taught in schools in certain subject areas. However they are far more powerful when woven into a single strand and applied across the curriculum. Recognizing these skills as combining together to form a united strategy, it is possible to make sense of the chaos of information out there – to change latent information into manifest information; in other words to convert raw data into useful knowledge.

I have used the word 'data' to describe raw unprocessed or latent information and 'information' to describe data that has been, processed or filtered in some way. That information can be refined in its turn until, selected and presented, it may become knowledge.

In Chapter 3 I suggest several options for simplifying the main skills into a memorable set of steps underpinned by the 20 skills. Used methodically throughout the education system this could be the foundation of every pupil *learning how to learn – for life*.

1
WHY IS INFORMATION LITERACY IMPORTANT?

And still they gaz'd and still the wonder grew,
That one small head could carry all he knew
.*(Goldsmith*, 'The Deserted Village', 1770)

Today even Goldsmith's village schoolmaster would be forced to Google to keep up with the ever-expanding quantity of knowledge. No one person – not even one library – today can be in the position of a 'Renaissance Man' or the Royal Library of Alexandria and know everything.

Samuel Johnson's definition:

Knowledge is of two kinds: we know a subject ourselves, or we know where to find information upon it.

clarifies this vital distinction. With more knowledge comes more specialism. Specialists with a deep knowledge of a very tiny area tend to lack the understanding of the interrelation of knowledge from different fields; generalists skate thinly over a broader but incomplete area, grasping superficial links between fields but lacking a depth of understanding. We cannot hold a fraction of the available knowledge in our heads at once, so we need to work in teams with a mixture of strengths and make further information available as necessary. We then need the skills of retrieving that information and making good use of it.

We recognize that a lot of information is actually duplicating or only slightly modifying an earlier source, but in that duplication lies redundancy – the ability to replace one source with another without losing the data.

Once, one could only copy the original by hand, which meant few copies and a high risk of total loss. The printing press's main purpose was to create copies and 500 years of improvements in printing created vast numbers of copies of a wide range of texts. Even in our online electronic age printed books continue to flourish. Personal computers, scanners and accessible software have continued the explosion and there can be few if any texts online that have not been copied somewhere, whether by the original publisher, the administrator, an archivist or by readers and users. So the problem of identifying the nuggets from the

10

mass of rock is harder than ever, but probably more important than ever.

The US Secretary of Defense Donald Rumsfeld famously said:

> there are known knowns; there are things we know we know. We also know there are known unknowns; that is to say we know there are some things we do not know. But there are also unknown unknowns – the ones we don't know we don't know.

He was much mocked for saying this, but unlike some of his other rather garbled quotations, this one is absolutely true of information. He takes the idea further than Samuel Johnson's two kinds of knowledge and extends it to include not only things we are aware of but don't understand (the 'known unknowns') but to the edge of unknowing (the 'unknown unknowns') beyond our understanding. In an age of information glut it's wise to acknowledge that however much information there is, there remain things we are not even aware of.

Core knowledge

There is certainly knowledge we must have ready at hand – basic facts, frequently used information and established knowledge which creates a framework around which we can fit new learning. 'What we know' is typically divided into a dozen traditional knowledge areas and includes key dates in history, important places in geography, grammatical 'rules' of English, basic calculations in mathematics and the periodic table in science. It also, most importantly, includes the *significance* of these events, places and facts so that we can build on them to create a more detailed, more relevant and up-to-date scheme for our world. The facts are important but even more important is the *understanding* of them, which includes their significance, the ability to connect and relate them and to apply the knowledge and perhaps even the appreciation and empathy that come with real understanding.

11

This book is about the essential skill of knowing how and where to find out more, so we can update, revise and build on our existing knowledge. We may learn essential facts and understand their significance while at school, and this provides the foundation framework. The curriculum is supposed to supply that framework in a logical way, methodically covering areas of learning which are important to our future.

The rest of our lives is spent in building upon that framework, using skills of selection, scrutiny, literacy and information technology to make sure the new knowledge sits in the right place in the framework. We need to be confident that the new information is correct and appropriate. Sometimes we need to unlearn things we have previously taken for granted and often this is more time-consuming than learning anew.

Along the way we may come to question the accepted divisions between areas of knowledge. We may develop new 'schemata' or 'constructs' – those internal representations of our world; an organization of concepts and actions that can be revised by new information about the world. And these developments, weighed against our prior knowledge and experience, help us to grow and to adapt to changes in the world around us.

Reliability

While our world is changing, the records of those changes – those new facts, observations, reflections and opinions – are expanding at a phenomenal rate. Crucially this information is becoming more accessible to us, no longer locked in chained libraries or the closed rooms of research laboratories. However at the same time as its accessibility increases, its reliability can decrease. Something given as a fact and publicized can be very quickly copied and sent around the world until it is generally believed – even if it has not been verified. Hence rumours and hoaxes, urban legends and conspiracy theories.

Hoaxes

- Nostradamus predicted 9/11
- The Good Times computer virus
- Chain letters about saving a dying child.

Urban legends

- Alligators live in the New York sewers.
- Kidney thieves are lurking ready to drug you and take a kidney to be sold on the black market.
- Granny dies and is tied to the roof rack of a car which is then stolen.

Conspiracy theories

- Dinosauroid-like alien reptiles from the constellation Draco are dominating the world.
- Apollo 11 moon landings were faked by NASA with CIA support.
- September 11 was orchestrated by the US Government.
- Barcodes are really intended to control people.
- A crashed alien spacecraft is kept in secret Area 51.

With the printing revolution of the fifteenth century and its expanding knowledge base of printed books came scope for writers to be read. Publishers and printers controlled this content and indexes; catalogues, encyclopedias and libraries made it easy to find. Information technology has changed the nature of formal publishing and printing but it has revolutionized informal publishing. First came desktop publishing, then globally accessible blogs, podcasts and web pages, automatically indexed by electronic assistants for internet search engines to be viewed on iPods, PDAs (Personal Digital Assistants), iPhones, electronic notebooks and laptops as well as desktop computers.

However, with every individual now a potential author acting as his own publisher, where are the editors and where are the librarians? The traditional publishing and editing system was a filter, and often a wise adviser. Today there is nothing between your thoughts and the world – which may be an advantage for self-expression but is a big problem for reliability.

Shelf guides for the global library

When I first accessed the internet, in 1994, I did so as a school librarian with an idea that here was a way to increase my library stock. What I found was a confused space, with no catalogue or organization, no editing or ranking.

Within weeks I realized that far from finding the solution to my problems, the solution had *become* the problem. That new problem, of how to make sense of this huge and growing mountain of information, is now more important than ever. Who is tidying the shelves in the global library? Who is throwing away the rubbish? Teachers and librarians have a great responsibility to help pupils to cope.

To take one example, the search engine company Google has undertaken the scanning of non-copyright books from the Bodleian and four other libraries so that these books are digitized and made available online. The advantages to readers and researchers are obvious – no more queuing at the library for books to be dug out for you, no fines for them being kept out too long, no librarian assistant apologizing that the library will be closing in ten minutes ... . Here, fast approaching, is the Great Library of the internet which may one day include 'the entire works of humankind, from the beginning of recorded history, in all languages, available to all people, all the time' writes Kevin Kelly, *New York Times*, 14 May 2006. 'From the days of Sumerian clay tablets till now, humans have "published" at least 32 million books, 750 million articles and essays, 25 million songs, 500 million images, 500,000 movies, 3 million videos, TV shows and short films and 100 billion public Web pages'.

And what if all this could be downloaded onto an iPod? You could carry the World's Library in your top pocket. That's how it felt to me when I first received the *Complete Oxford English Dictionary* on a single CD-Rom. The real issue then is: What are you going to do with it? How do you search it, browse it, trawl through it and make sense of what's there? What good are all these riches if you can't synthesize or apply the knowledge hidden within or separate the gems from the rest of the mountain?

The knowledge economy

If knowledge is power, then the ability to publish, access and disseminate knowledge is the most powerful force of all. We must, therefore, learn these skills ourselves, and ensure our pupils learn them too.

Knowledge is also a route to riches. Eighteenth-century England was a mainly rural economy, shaken up in the nineteenth century by an industrial revolution which used local natural resources to create goods with added value. New skills were needed. Ploughmen became loom operators and iron smelters. Soon local resources were replaced by materials from elsewhere, including the Empire. Iron smelters became ships' boiler makers. By the second half of the twentieth century UK manufactured goods were being eclipsed by cheaper goods produced in Hong Kong, Korea and Japan. Shipyard workers became salesmen. By the turn of the twenty-first century traditional manual trades such as steel and coal production had virtually ceased in the UK and the skills needed by school leavers were no longer in ship-building but more likely to be in the service industries and in that new creation, the Knowledge Economy. It is here that information literacy is most needed.

A vital part of our economy is based around providing, assessing, packaging and selling on the commodity we know as information. There are librarians, pollsters, database managers, investment traders, journalists, publishers, media personalities, meteorologists, scientists and IT specialists of all kinds researching, sorting, discriminating, assessing, evaluating, publishing, presenting, marketing and selling news, statistics, data, opinion, advice, etc. based on information gleaned and gathered from all corners of the earth and targeted at consumers. We have in a large part become a knowledge-based economy.

And we are competing globally with other countries and economies. Australia trades more goods with Asia and Japan than with the UK, but its news gatherers and online businesses trade worldwide via an internet that gives everyone with broadband access the same opportunity to contact anyone else irrespective of where they are. Apart from differences in local time zones I can contact someone on the other side of the globe as easily as the person in the next town. I can promptly supply information which is up to date and accurate and has the benefit of local knowledge and receive similar information in return. I can produce a website in Perth, Western Australia that is instantly visible in Perth, Scotland or Perth Amboy, New Jersey. I can produce part of a newspaper or book on one continent, send it to another where local news is added and have the combined publication printed or published online on a third continent or on several continents simultaneously. Have we prepared our students for this?

Information literacy is more than just looking up a word in a book or entering it into a search engine and reading 'the answer'. We must learn to phrase our question appropriately, define our terms and inspect a variety of answers.

Comparing sources

How do you make sense of the following information?

Example 1 Quiz

<u>Question</u> Where does the word 'quiz' come from?
<u>Answer A</u> 'Origin unknown', (Encarta World Dictionary).
<u>Answer B</u> 'There is a famous tall tale about a Dublin theatre

---

manager, who accepted a bet that he could create a new word without any meaning and have everybody in the city using it within 24 hours. He paid children to go around the city chalking the word quiz everywhere so that the next day everybody was asking what this word meant' (several websites).

Answer C 'This picturesque tale appeared as an anecdote in 1836, but the most detailed account (in F. T. Porter's *Gleanings and Reminiscences*, 1875) gives the date of the exploit as 1791. The word, however, was already in use by then, meaning "an odd or eccentric person", and had been used in this sense by Fanny Burney in her diary on 24 June 1782' (AskOxford.com).

In this case it was necessary to look at several sources and not to simply choose the first one. We may not now know the ultimate answer, or even the date, but we have several pieces of information from which to make a choice.

We may make that choice on the basis of the reputation of the source, whether sources agree or even the way the source expresses itself. AskOxford quotes its own sources and has a reputation for thoroughness so is the most likely answer here.

Where there is a mass of uncoordinated information much of it is likely to conflict. Even where it all seems to agree there is a chance it all comes from the same false source. Cross-checking sources is essential for serious information users such as journalists, police and researchers. They know that information can be wrong and they try to distinguish between rumour and reliable sources. They try to allow for prejudice and bias.

It's also possible for one person to make an error and for that error to be multiplied many times across the internet. Matthew Parris, writing in *The Times* on 15 November 2007, said he quoted Graham Greene that 'the mark of a really cruel man is that he cries in the cinema'. A friend of his claimed the quotation was by Goebbels. A Google search showed all the references to this quotation linked back to Parris himself, with no corroborating evidence. So if he was wrong, everyone's got it wrong ....

Conclusion: cross-check sources for reliability.

Example 2 Is the Peppered Moth an example of evolution or creationism?

In 1953 and 1955 Bernard Kettlewell carried out experiments on the Peppered Moth. He suggested that the Peppered Moth population became darker with an increase in industrial pollution because the dark moths were better hidden against black polluted trees and survived more successfully than the lighter moths, which were more easily found and eaten by birds. This was generally held to be a classic example of natural selection.

However some people believe that God created the world. These creationists express views very different from the Darwinian evolutionists. We should bear this in mind while reading the following information sources.

Source 1
www.arn.org/docs/wells/jw_pepmoth.htm
This is an apparently well-argued scientific analysis by Jonathan Wells of the evidence so far. It agrees that the science was mistaken but does not conclude that there was any deliberate intention to mislead.
Source 2
www.bible.ca/tracks/textbook-fraud-pepper-moth-biston-betularia.htm
This page argues that evolutionists have little worthwhile to say: they believe they can rebut the evolutionist argument because 'The pepper moth is not valid science'. This article also quotes extracts from the Jonathan Wells article above.
Source 3
The scientific community has defended the teaching of evolution in US public schools and has expressed its view as 'responses to Jonathan Wells' in brief at
www.ncseweb.org/resources/articles/
7719_responses_to_jonathan_wells3_11_28_2001.asp
Source 4
Wikipedia www.biocrawler.com/encyclopedia/Peppered_moth
says: 'Beginning in 1998, the traditional peppered moth story

> has been criticised by several people, but most prominently by creationists. "All the peppered-moth pictures were staged," said biologist Jonathan Wells, a senior fellow at the Discovery Institute. "Scientists have known since the 1980s that the moths do not normally rest on tree trunks."'
> Wikipedia comments that 'The scientific community remains unimpressed'.

What do we know of these sources?

Source 1 is from a website proposing the theory of 'Intelligent Design' which is a non-scientific belief in an unnamed God.

Source 2 is from a Christian foundation which proposes the creationist theory. The URL links to www.bible.ca/false.htm which is a list of 'false doctrines' that apparently contradict the Bible. The site uses these so-called false beliefs to demonstrate what the writers say is the true belief.

Source 3 is seen from a scientific perspective.

Source 4 Wikipedia is an open-source encyclopedia which is scrutinized and edited by users. It notes that several of the scientists referred to in Jonathan Wells' book have said that they were quoted out of context or that their work has been misrepresented.

Noticing whether the URL includes an academic (ac or edu) suffix or a biblical word (bible.ca in Source 2) is a useful clue to site references in this case. Triangulating sources by comparing and contrasting at least three is always useful, but in Examples 2 and 3 there are so many sites that it would be easy to find three in agreement for either point of view. A useful strategy in this example would be to click 'pages from the UK' in www.google.co.uk/ because many of the creationist sites are US in origin and this would filter them out.

There are clear differences between the scientific evolutionists and the creationist Bible followers. Prejudice obviously plays its part – often more so than evidence.

Conclusion: check all sources for prejudice and reliability.

Example 3 Were dinosaurs on Noah's Ark?

Source 1
www.answersingenesis.org/docs2001/dinos_on_ark.asp
The story we have all heard is that dinosaurs 'ruled the Earth'
for 140 million years, died out 65 million years ago, and
therefore weren't around when Noah and company set sail on
the Ark around 4,300 years ago. However, the Bible gives a
completely different view of Earth (and therefore, dinosaur)
history. As God's written Word to us, we can trust it to tell the
truth about the past.

Source 2
www.biblicalgeology.net/
'For the purposes of the geological model we use the dates
published by Ussher, rounded to the nearest 100 years. The
flood is taken as occurring in 2300 BC, and creation in 4000 BC.'
    It was Archbishop James Ussher who in the 1650s put
forward the idea that the creation of the world occurred in
4004 BC.

Source 3
The Natural History Museum in London has a site called the
Dino Directory http://internt.nhm.ac.uk/jdsml/nature-online/
dino-directory/timeline.dsml?disp = gall&sort = Genus
with a timeline showing dinosaurs from the Upper Triassic
period back to 227 million years ago. Dinosaurs from the
middle Jurassic period are dated between 159 and 180 million
years ago.

Again there are clearly two different points of view and the
evidence has been interpreted completely differently. In Source 1
and Source 2 creationists start from the point of view that the
Bible is the Word of God and so must be true, while in Source 3
evolutionists use an evidence-based scientific approach.

    Conclusion: distinguish between firmly held belief and
scientific fact.

Example 4 What is the capital of Assyria?

Answer 1 Four capitals of Assyria were Ashur (or Qalat Sherqat), Calah (or Kalakh, or Nimrud), the short-lived Dur Sharrukin (or Khorsabad) and Nineveh. The ruins of all four ancient cities fall within the modern state of Iraq.

Answer 2 In The Ancient Near East c.3000–330 BC by Amélie Kuhrt (1995) after conquest by Alexander the Great, 'Asyria proper, with its capital Arbela, was variously known as Hdayab (Syriac), Adiabene (Greek and Latin), Nôd-Šîragân (Parthian) and Ardaxširagân (Sassanid Persian). Even today, the Christian church of Adiabene, which is very old, still calls itself Assyrian.'

Here sources are less important than the precise nature of the question. The historical periods, varying geography, different languages and written forms all make it impossible to give a single simple answer. The question is incorrect to assume there is one answer.

Conclusion: the question affects the answer; frequently there is no simple answer – 'it depends'.

Different views

In these examples adults may understand that there are two very different views, but children may accept the first answer given to them. It is our role as teachers to show the difference between fact and opinion and that even in the realms of fact that there can be different points of view and different interpretations of the same evidence. They need to look for evidence to support the case and to weigh it in the light of who is giving us that evidence and in what context.

Not only is there a mass of information out there, but it is sometimes impenetrable and often contradictory. Life isn't as simple as those who are looking for 'the answer' would like it to be.

Information skills aim to clarify the process. How we teach that process starts with the school curriculum.

2
INFORMATION LITERACY SKILLS ACROSS THE CURRICULUM

What are the skills used in handling information? The terminology is sometimes inconsistent so common ground between school subject areas is not always obvious. For example 'Ask appropriate questions' in geography would be similar to 'Specify the problem' in mathematics and 'Discuss and question critically' in art. Similarly, 'Evaluation' might be described as 'be clear about what you have achieved' in physical education and 'suggest improvements' in science.

Chapter 3 covers each of the main 20 skills in some detail, but this chapter is concerned with how individual subjects in a subject-based curriculum can address areas of importance to their own academic study while contributing to the whole curriculum. It is only by working together on a methodical strategy with a common aim that our pupils will see how information skills pervade the whole curriculum.

The Information Literacy Strand

Where references to information literacy are dispersed through-out the school curriculum we can refer to this as a strand. The Information Literacy Strand weaves its way in and out of all subject areas, sometimes obviously, sometimes less so.

What is significant about this undervalued strand in the curriculum?

- First, the fact that this strand exists (even if it is hidden in places) demonstrates the importance of these skills in the modern school curriculum.
- Second, the fact that it is present in all main subject areas shows how relevant it is to education in the round. Even where 'education' is broken into traditional curriculum headings, information skills are everywhere and can serve to unify a sometimes fragmented curriculum.
- Third, since these skills must be taught, it makes sense for them to be taught in cooperation, with subject teachers teaching skills and creating learning opportunities in the knowledge that their colleagues are similarly active and the

whole school is working together. Teachers build on each other's work and 'spiral upwards'.

- Finally, when individuals and departments can come together to agree on what skills will be taught where, it is possible to squeeze more into the limited time available.

It is possible to see information literacy as a force for breaking down barriers between traditional subjects. Secondary schools/ high schools are particularly firm about what is and what is not their subject. These schools could learn from the teaching of younger pupils in which learning crosses boundaries, whatever label is placed on it, often helped by a single teacher for whom 'subjects' are useful labels, not barriers. Young pupils must be baffled to move from a school where a topic-based on a skills-based curriculum allows learning to roam freely, to a school where knowledge is taught in tight blocks and contact between blocks is frowned upon. In too many schools it is simply unacceptable that English and mathematics or English and science should ever share knowledge and teach joined-up learning . . ..

Information literacy is an essential set of skills common to all subject areas – and this need not mean it adds to the burden of the curriculum. These skills are already contained within our curriculum; information literacy seeks to bring existing skills together, make them coherent and make them explicit to our pupils. If all subject areas teach these skills then each is helping the others to collectively improve pupils' abilities.

In 2007, for implementation from September 2008, the National Curriculum for England and Wales underwent revision. Edited extracts from those Curriculum documents relating to information literacy are arranged by age group and by subject below. In the left-hand column is the National Curriculum target (www.nytimes.com/2006/05/14/magazine/14publishing.html); the right-hand column has examples by the present author relating specifically to information and research tasks.

National Curriculum and examples

National Curriculum Key Stage 2 (aged 8–11) – Information Skills Strand

Most National Curriculum subjects at this stage refer to aspects of information skills. Those that do not provide opportunities to include it if desired.

Recurrent words describing information skills at this stage include:

- ask and answer questions
- record
- communicate
- work with a range of information
- organize
- reflect
- choose
- select.

Extracts from Programmes of Study	Suggested examples
Art and Design	
- Record from experience and imagination, to select and record ...	Create your own Art Gallery. Teacher uses Google image search (set on Safe Search) to help find suitable images from which pupils select and write their own commentary. They could include references to the original and its creator and present the whole as a slide show.
- Question and make thoughtful observations	
Citizenship	
- Research, discuss and debate topical issues, problems and events	Research any topical issue. Use the SWOT analysis grid (see 'Problem solving' in Chapter 3

and Appendix 5) and the Argument Table (see 'Sorting and arranging' in Chapter 3 and Appendix 9).
Write pros and cons and main issues in bullet-point style.
Use the collected ideas for a debate or a wall display of the main arguments.

Design & Technology

- Generate ideas for products after thinking about who will use them and what they will be used for, using information from a number of sources, including ICT-based sources

- Communicate design ideas in different ways

- Investigating and evaluating a range of familiar products, thinking about how they work, how they are used and the views of the people who use them

Design a combined sleep and study zone for your bedroom. Research existing solutions using catalogues, visiting shops, viewing websites and identifying the pros and cons of each solution before creating your own answer.
If possible, interview people who have lived with one of the existing solutions and include their responses.

English

- Choose material that is relevant to the topic and to the listeners

- Identify the gist of an account or key points

Produce a set of book reviews written by the class and share them with other classes.
Give the pupils the opportunity to respond to the reviews. This can be done on a Virtual Learning Environment using a

- The range of purposes should include:
  a. investigating, selecting, sorting
  b. planning, predicting, exploring
  c. explaining, reporting, evaluating.

discussion tool, on an online blog or on paper in a loose leaf folder.

Geography

- Collect and record evidence

- Analyse evidence and draw conclusions

- Communicate in ways appropriate to the task and audience

- To use atlases and globes, and maps and plans at a range of scales (for example, using contents, keys, grids, etc.)

- To use secondary sources of information, including aerial photographs (for example, stories, information texts, the internet, satellite images, photographs, videos)

Local study.
The study could be of housing types, front gardens, green areas, etc. The evidence could be written, drawn, photographed, etc.
Evidence could be linked to aerial photographs (Google Earth) and compared with evidence from another locality provided by another school, or by research – for example using the neighbourhood profiles at Up My Street at www.upmystreet.com.
Build up a fact file of an area, based on the ordinance survey mapped photographs at www.geograph.org.uk.

History

- How to find out about the events, people and changes studied from an appropriate range of sources of information, including ICT-based sources (for example,

Local libraries usually keep a local history section.
Interview older local residents.
Use a local war memorial to research World War I
using the Commonwealth War

27

documents, printed sources,
CD-ROMS, databases, pictures
and photographs, music,
artefacts, historic buildings
and visits to museums,
galleries and sites)

- To ask and answer questions,
and to select and record
information relevant to the
focus of the enquiry

Information and Communications Technology

- To talk about what
information pupils need and
how they can find and use it
(for example, searching the
internet or a CD-ROM, using
printed material, asking
people)

- How to develop and refine
ideas by bringing together,
organizing and reorganizing
text, tables, images and
sound as appropriate (for
example, desktop publishing,
multimedia presentations)

- How to share and exchange
information in a variety of
forms, including email (for
example, displays, posters,
animations, musical
compositions)

- To be sensitive to the needs
of the audience and think

Graves website at www.cwgc.org
Use *The Times* searchable
database to produce a timeline
of significant events (this may
be accessed using your local
library card).

Using any of the ideas listed
elsewhere, rehearse the skills of:

- searching
- selective copy and paste
- editing
- creating hyperlinks
- creating web pages
- presenting slide shows
- adding sound and video clips
- combining multimedia
  resources.

Discuss the pros and cons of
different media and how they
can be used most effectively
for different purposes.

carefully about the content and quality when communicating information (for example, work for presentation to other pupils, writing for parents, publishing on the internet)

- Working with a range of information to consider its characteristics and purposes (for example, collecting factual data from the internet and a class survey to compare the findings)

- Working with others to explore a variety of information sources and ICT tools (for example, searching the internet for information about a different part of the world, designing textile patterns using graphics software, using ICT tools to capture and change sounds)

Mathematics

- Organize work and refine ways of recording
- Use notation diagrams and symbols correctly

Create flow diagrams for complex problems.
Create spreadsheets to calculate the requirements for a party, a holiday or a tuck shop.
Vary the conditions, the number of people, amount of money available, etc., and check how the spreadsheet copes with the changes.

Modern Foreign Languages

- Pupils are beginning to use dictionaries or glossaries to check words they have learnt

Compile a phrase book for a particular event or situation. Include labelled pictures of vocabulary items. Try it out with role play then modify the phrase book accordingly.

Science

- Ask questions that can be investigated scientifically and decide how to find answers
- Consider what sources of information, including first-hand experience and a range of other sources, pupils will use to answer questions
- Think about what might happen or try things out when deciding what to do, what kind of evidence to collect and what equipment and materials to use
- Use a wide range of methods, including diagrams, drawings, tables, bar charts, line graphs and ICT, to communicate data in an appropriate and systematic manner

Compile a class list of suitable scientific questions.
If it helps, visit 'Common science question and answers' at sciencepage.org/question.htm.

Pupils can research answers explained using principles the pupils themselves can understand. Often if the questions are about processes or events the answers can be expressed well using storyboards or the software Comic Life by Plasq.com.

Religious Education

- Use and interpret information about religions from a range of sources

Use the BBC Multi-Faith Calendar at www.bbc.co.uk/religion/tools/calendar/ to produce your own calendar with graphics and explanations of events.

Personal, Social and Health Education

– To research, discuss and debate topical issues, problems and events	Research any topical issue. Use the SWOT analysis grid (see 'Problem solving' in Chapter 3 and Appendix 5) and the
– Find information and advice (for example, through helplines; by understanding about welfare systems in society)	Argument Table (see 'Sorting and arranging' in Chapter 4 and Appendix 9). Research and evaluate the best information sources for a personal issue and compile a directory to guide young people who need help.

National Curriculum Key Stage 3 (aged 12–14) – Information Skills Strand

Below are edited extracts relevant to information skills from the 2008 National Curriculum for England and Wales, for children aged 12–14 (my emphasis) http://curriculum.qca.org.uk/subjects/index.aspx.

Successful learners

These pupils:

– have the essential learning skills of literacy, numeracy and *information and communication* technology
– are creative, resourceful and able to *identify and solve problems*
– have enquiring minds and *think for themselves to process information, reason, question and evaluate*
– communicate well in a range of ways
– *understand how they learn* and learn from their mistakes
– are *able to learn independently* and with others
– know about big ideas and events that shape our world
– enjoy learning and are motivated to achieve the best they can now and in the future.

Functional skills

Functional skills are those core elements of English, mathematics and ICT that provide an individual with the essential knowledge, skills and understanding that will enable them to operate confidently, effectively and independently in life and at work. Individuals at any age who possess these skills will be able to participate and progress in education, training and employment as well as develop and secure the broader range of aptitudes, attitudes and behaviours that will enable them to make a positive contribution to the communities in which they live and work.

In English

Each individual will be able to read and understand information and instructions, then use this understanding to act appropriately and to analyse how ideas and information are presented, evaluating their usefulness, for example in solving a problem. They will be able to make an oral presentation or report, contribute to discussions and use speech to work collaboratively to agree actions and conclusions.

In Information and Communications Technology

Pupils will use ICT to find, select and bring together relevant information and to develop, interpret and exchange information, for a purpose.

Key processes, Key Stage 3 (aged 12–14)

Most National Curriculum subjects at this stage refer to aspects of information skills. Those that do not provide opportunities to include it if desired. To the following extracts from National Curriculum Programmes of Study I have added some suggested activities.

Extracts from Programmes of Study	Suggested examples

Art and Design

2.2a use research and investigative skills appropriate to art, craft and design	Research the background to an artist's method, choice of materials and influences.
2.2d analyse, select and question critically	Explain your findings in a presentation or an annotated
2.2f organize and present their own material and information in appropriate forms.	wall display.

Citizenship

2.1 Critical thinking and enquiry	Research any topical issue. Use the SWOT analysis grid (see 'Problem solving in Chapter 3 and Appendix 5) and the
a engage with and reflect on different ideas, opinions, beliefs and values when exploring topical and controversial issues and problems	argument table (see 'Sorting and arranging' in Chapter 3 and Appendix 9). Write pros and cons and main issues in bullet-point style.
b research, plan and undertake enquiries into issues and problems using a range of information and sources	Try to attribute views to groups of people or belief systems. Use this to identify prejudices and search for similar prejudices
c analyse and evaluate sources used, questioning different values, ideas and viewpoints and recognizing bias.	by the same people and groups in other topics. Use the collected ideas for a debate or a wall display of the main arguments.

Design & Technology

2a generate, develop, model and communicate ideas in a range of ways, using appropriate strategies	First research different inexpensive home barbecues and pay particular attention to the way they are advertised to the customer.

Now research different high-performance cars, again noting the way they are presented to potential customers.

Finally, try the presentation methods of the car to advertise the barbecue. Does it work? What do we learn?

English

2.2 Reading, Reading for meaning

a extract and interpret information, events, main points and ideas from texts
b infer and deduce meanings, recognizing the writers' intentions
c understand how meaning is constructed within sentences and across texts as a whole
d select and compare information from different texts
e assess the usefulness of texts, sift the relevant from the irrelevant and distinguish between fact and opinion
f recognize and discuss different interpretations of texts, justifying their [pupils'] own views on what they read and see, and supporting them with evidence
g understand how audiences and readers choose and respond to texts

Study the news for a single day using a range of newspapers, TV news broadcasts, radio stations and internet sites. What is emphasized and what is not said? What is explored at length? What is hinted at but not said specifically? How is this expressed?

Use the material linguistically to look at cliché, how the form of a news story differs from other literary forms, how people are described, etc.

Use this research as the background for a News Day where a class or a year group produce a newspaper (or series of web pages or a TV news broadcast) based on real news including local stories.

A deadline of a single day is important in introducing a sense of excitement and purpose.

h understand how the nature
and purpose of texts
influences the selection of
content and its meanings

i understand how meaning is
created through the
combination of words, images
and sounds in multimodal
texts.

Geography

2.1 Geographical enquiry

a ask geographical questions,
thinking critically,
constructively and creatively

b collect, record and display
information

c identify bias, opinion and
abuse of evidence in sources
when investigating issues

d analyse and evaluate evidence,
presenting findings to draw
and justify conclusions

e find creative ways of using
and applying geographical
skills and understanding to
create new interpretations of
place and space

f plan geographical enquiries,
suggesting appropriate
sequences of investigation

g solve problems and make
decisions to develop
analytical skills and creative
thinking about geographical
issues.

Propose a hypothesis about
settlements or transport networks
(why they are situated here,
why they link these places, etc.)
and use Google Earth to do
aerial surveys to collect evidence
to support your hypothesis.
Compare this aerial evidence
with other evidence – your own
study of the ground or the
evidence and research of others.
Does this evidence support your
hypothesis, or otherwise?

Compile meteorological data
from satellite pictures, the Met
Office and Google Earth to show
weather patterns and the effects
of this weather on the ground.
Explain how this information
can help predict future weather
– and why that prediction is so
difficult.

2.3 Graphicacy and visual
literacy

a use atlases, globes, maps at a
   range of scales, photographs,
   satellite images and other
   geographical data
b construct maps and plans at a
   variety of scales, using graphical
   techniques to present evidence.

History

2.1 Historical enquiry

a identify and investigate,
   individually and as part of a
   team, specific historical
   questions or issues, making
   and testing hypotheses.

2.2 Using evidence

a identify, select and use a
   range of historical sources,
   including textual, visual and
   oral sources, artefacts and the
   historic environment
b evaluate the sources used in
   order to reach reasoned
   conclusions.

Interview an old person from
your community who has lived
in the area for a long time.
What was life like in their day?
What do they remember that
has been lost, changed,
demolished? How is life different?
Follow this up with research in
old newspapers, books of local
history, old postcards,
photographs, etc.
Where possible compare with
another elderly resident.
Though this is ideal homework
some teachers find it easier to
invite someone in to the classroom to be interviewed by a
group and perhaps videoed.
Present the results to the class
and to old residents themselves.

Information and Communication Technology

2.1 Finding information

a consider systematically the
   information needed to solve
   a problem, complete a task

Many of the other research
tasks suggested elsewhere will
make use of ICT.
In order to try out some of
the wide range of available

or answer a question, and explore how it will be used

b use and refine search methods to obtain information that is well matched to purpose, by selecting appropriate sources

c collect and enter quantitative and qualitative information, checking its accuracy

d analyse and evaluate information, judging its value, accuracy, plausibility and bias.

software, compile a set of reviews of useful organizing and enhancing software then publicize it on the school website.

Some interesting and helpful software is given elsewhere.

2.2 Developing ideas

a select and use ICT tools and techniques appropriately, safely and efficiently

b solve problems by developing, exploring and structuring information, and deriving new information for a particular purpose

d design information systems and suggest improvements to existing systems

f bring together, draft and refine information, including through the combination of text, sound and image.

2.3 Communicating information

a use a range of ICT tools to present information in forms that are fit for purpose, meet audience needs and suit the content.

Mathematics

2.1d select mathematical information, methods and tools to use

2.3c be aware of the strength of empirical evidence and appreciate the difference between evidence and proof

2.3d look at data to find patterns and exceptions

National Statistics Online www.statistics.gov.uk/ is a website holding all manner of statistics relating to the UK. FedStats www.fedstats.gov/ and the US Census Bureau www.census.gov/ have similar up-to-date statistical banks. Present these statistics in a variety of ways using charts and graphical devices to assess the most effective ways of delivering a statistical message. Printed periodicals also frequently use graphics to present statistical information to less numerate readers.

Modern Foreign Languages

2.1e use reference materials such as dictionaries appropriately and effectively

2.2b skim and scan written texts for the main points or details

Research the town your school uses for its exchange programme and write or film a simple bilingual guide to its main features.

Music

2.2a analyse, review, evaluate and compare pieces of music

Research reviews of musical pieces, both performances and recordings. Contrast reviews of the same performance. Compare and contrast 'cover versions' of popular songs.

Personal Social and Health Education

Economic well-being

2.2 Exploration

Use some of the careers tools such as JIGCAL, which offers

a use a variety of information sources to explore options and choices in career and financial contexts
b recognize bias and inaccuracies in information about learning pathways, work and enterprise.

Personal well-being
2.2 Decision making and managing risk

a use knowledge and understanding to make informed choices about safety, health and well-being
b find information and support from a variety of sources.

Physical Education
Information skills are not explicitly stated in the Curriculum Processes but PE provides many opportunities to ask questions, solve problems, test a hypothesis, research alternatives and the many skills of information processing.

a route through a maze of careers information.
Compile your own flow diagram to show the route you have travelled so far and the possible routes to be followed in the future. This diagram could be annotated with references and with questions designed to help others decide on suitable career routes.

Throwing, catching, running, jumping, swimming and dancing involve executing movements open to analysis, criticism, comparison and potential improvement.
Ask questions such as – could this be more effective, how could it generate more thrust, lift or exert more power with less energy are fundamental to improvement.
Recording performance and making comparisons with those of others can be simple observation and communication or lead to complex analysis,

39

involving research, understanding of dynamics and anatomy, reading the research of others and evaluating their work in your own context.

In Games, research on rules and on tactics is fundamental to an understanding of sport.

Related issues of health, diet and fitness require research and balancing and evaluating of different strategies and opinions.

Religious Education

2.1 Learning about religion

Use the BBC Multi-Faith Calendar at www.bbc.co.uk/religion/tools/calendar/ to produce your own calendar with graphics and explanations of events.

a investigate the impact of religious beliefs and teachings on individuals, communities and societies, the reasons for commitment and the causes of diversity

Include a piece for each event showing its origins and how celebration enriches the believers of that religion.

e interpret a range of sources, texts, authorities, and forms of religious and spiritual expression from a variety of contexts

f analyse religious beliefs, arguments and ideas.

Science

2.2 Critical understanding of evidence

Look beyond the headlines and at a number of sources (popular journals as well as popular newspapers) and compare their scientific interpretations of natural phenomena. Do the explanations by scientific advisors

a obtain, record and analyse data from a wide range of primary and secondary sources, including ICT

40

| sources, and use their findings to provide evidence for scientific explanations
b evaluate scientific evidence and working methods. | support or contradict the eye-catching headlines? Do scientists agree or disagree? Do they use science to support their arguments? |

To all of these we may add *communication, evaluation* and *reflection*.

The England and Wales Primary Literacy Strategy, launched in the DfES document (2003) *Excellence and Enjoyment – A Strategy for Primary Schools,* builds on the National Literacy Strategy, which lays out targets for literacy in some detail.

It is clear that finding out, asking questions, predicting events from information given and organizing and communicating answers are skills built in to the strategy from its earliest stages.

There is a specific Research and Study Skills Strand in the Framework for Teaching English (Years 7, 8 and 9) for England and Wales.

The Research and Study Skills Strand of the English National Literacy Strategy KS3 (age 12–14)

Pupils should be taught to:

Year 7

1. know how to locate resources for a given task, and find relevant information in them, e.g. skimming, use of index, glossary, key words, hotlinks
2. use appropriate reading strategies to extract particular information, e.g. highlighting, scanning
3. compare and contrast the ways information is presented in different forms, e.g. web pages, diagrams, prose
4. make brief, clearly organized notes of key points for later use
5. appraise the value and relevance of information found and acknowledge sources.

41

Year 8

1. combine information from various sources into one coherent document
2. undertake independent research using a range of reading strategies, applying their knowledge of how texts and ICT databases are organized and acknowledging sources
3. make notes in different ways, choosing a form which suits the purpose, e.g. diagrammatic notes, making notes during a video, abbreviating for speed and ease of retrieval.

Year 9

1. review and extend their own strategies for locating, appraising and extracting relevant information
2. synthesize information from a range of sources, shaping material to meet the reader's needs
3. increase the speed and accuracy of note-making skills and use notes for re-presenting information for specific purposes; evaluate the relevance, reliability and validity of information available through print, ICT and other media sources.

Here the skills are more elaborate and the descriptions are more detailed. They relate clearly to the 20 skills (see Chapter 3) and to the Nine Question Steps while building on the skills described in the Primary Strategy.

Note also that although they clearly relate to literacy, they do not refer specifically to any subject areas. These are cross-curricular skills, as valuable to the arts as the sciences, practical as well as academic skills. Life skills, in fact.

If you are a teacher you will probably recognize most of the curriculum references given above, even if you follow a different curriculum. They are typical of the sorts of things being taught in classrooms around the world. They are also important aspects of information literacy. In fact you may think that information literacy was there all the time, even though you may not have noticed it.

Since some subjects seem to have many targets relating to

information, you may ask why the others need to bother. My response is that every teacher is a teacher of learning. How our pupils learn shouldn't change when they move into someone else's classroom. If we are to teach pupils how to learn not just for now but for their future, they need to know how to learn for themselves. And that involves asking the right questions, finding the right answers and evaluating the information they use. It also means making the process explicit so pupils don't see this skill in your lesson in isolation but see it as part of a joined-up process.

As you teach these skills in relation to your history or your geography lesson, so the pupil is learning something that can be applied to your colleague's English or PE lesson as well as to the rest of the pupil's life. We are all teachers of learning. And if we teach our pupils how to find out now, they could be using that skill for the whole of their working lives. The child entering school in 2008 may not retire until 2063. We simply don't know what they will have to face then. The best way to future proof their education is to teach them how to learn, and teach them how to find out, which is just one part of how to learn.

Naturally curriculum aims and priorities differ from country to country, state to state and school to school. Nevertheless the references above will be relevant to most teachers of these subject areas and many teachers will find relevance in other subject areas too. No one subject has a monopoly on the teaching of information skills. I take it as self-evident that if you teach a skill in your lesson a different teacher can build on that skill in another lesson. This is consolidation, not duplication, and the clear winner is the pupil.

Any lesson can benefit from a little research or a simple run through of the steps of asking a question and finding out the answer. The teacher need not – and I would say *should* not – have the answers to every question. Below are some more extensive activities which can be adapted to suit any year group and topic.

Curriculum activities using information literacy

If these activities are put in the department curriculum documents and on the school timetable as recurring events they will have more impact than one-off activities. Embedding projects in the school curriculum means, in the very best sense, that they will be taken for granted – accepted as a useful and planned way of encouraging and developing information skills. With a bit of luck people will even look forward to it!

WebQuests

A *WebQuest* is a kind of guided internet treasure hunt. Good WebQuests help pupils discover for themselves, instead of being told. The choice of topic is almost infinite.

- They can let pupils work at their own pace, either individually or in teams.
- They let pupils explore selected areas in more depth, but within boundaries that you the teacher have selected.
- They are ideal for differentiated learning.
- They demonstrate the value of research, and practise the skills of finding out.

Most WebQuests have the following six steps:

1. *Introduction* – The stimulus material that grabs the pupils' interest and involves them with the task. It could be a real-life situation or a fantasy scenario.
2. *Task* – This could take a variety of formats and should have a realistic and achievable outcome.
3. *Process* – The WebQuest guides the pupil through the process. Pupils can work individually or as part of a larger group with individually assigned roles.
   The process will provide guidance on how to complete the task.
4. *Resources* – A WebQuest uses the internet as its main, though

not only, resource bank. Links from a main page guide pupils to the most appropriate resources, which can be differentiated and appropriate to ability.

5. *Evaluation* – The criteria on which pupils' work will be assessed, is presented here. Pupils can review what they are doing and judging the standard they are achieving by comparing with other successful work.

6. *Conclusion* – Finally pupils can evaluate their progress and either revise what they have done or explore further.

Teachers First – Putting Discovery into the Curriculum
www.teachersfirst.com/summer/webquest/quest-a.shtml
WebQuests UK www.webquestuk.org.uk/

The Radio Days WebQuest
The task is described as follows:

> You are an employee of a local radio station. Your boss, who grew up during the 'Golden Age' of radio, has decided to add new programming to the station. He has assigned you and your co-workers the task of writing and producing a new radio drama. Your boss expects you and your co-workers to research the history of radio drama and use this knowledge to create a script for a new radio mystery/suspense series. He wants the script to contain references to sound effects as well as the actors' dialogue. In addition to the script, you and your team are to present a recorded demo-version of the play, complete with sound effects.

The WebQuest goes on to define the roles for the members of the group, suggests the steps and timing you have to go through and gives resources for you to use.

The Radio Days WebQuest www.thematzats.com/radio/

Plan a Holiday

Plan a Holiday is an information skills task, similar to a WebQuest, for pupils at Key Stage 3–4. Through the activity of planning a holiday for themselves and their friends to celebrate the end of their examinations pupils have to progress through the main steps of information handling. They use the skills of information literacy to determine their task, find sources of information, sort and arrange the information to match the task, then make a presentation to the rest of the group on what they've discovered – and where the group will go for their joint holiday.

Plan a Holiday www.putlearningfirst.com/holiday/

Local studies research

A local study is an ideal topic for cross-curricular work. With history and geography as the main focus, English, mathematics and science all have a role to play in researching, enquiring and presenting findings. A local study can be tailored to almost any need as you can see from the following list of possibilities:

English Writing diaries past and present. Comparing the language of old newspapers with current language styles. Creating a soap opera drama starting from the known historic facts of people and houses within the settlement.

Geography Population growth, occupations of those who worked in the settlement and how these have changed, industry versus agriculture, functions of the settlement and land use. Mapping exercises and transects. Visit Google Earth for aerial views.

History Why is this settlement here? How did it develop and why? What records are there of its growth and/or decline? Look at maps, census returns, births, marriages and deaths. Visit www.1837online.com/ Interview local people. Look at remaining buildings, architectural style, dates. Read old newspapers, trade directories, parish registers, family trees, churchyard memorials.

ICT Methodical research of existing websites. Creation of pages for the school website presenting all the findings. Design and creation of a database to collect the data. Processing photographs of the settlement, linking them to a map with 'hot spots' and explanatory text.

Mathematics Analysis of numerical data – census returns, population growth – and creation of charts.

Science Pupils should have the opportunity to experience science outside the school environment, including in the workplace, where possible. A scientific audit could be made of the local area to show how science has an extensive range of influences. Pupils could use scientific categories such as energy and electricity, chemicals and materials, organisms and health, the environment and the earth to identify key processes used in the workplace or the local area. Looking at energy use in the urban environment, chemicals in agriculture, domestic energy use in heating and lighting, etc., there is scope for further research and for comparing modern-day use with the same area 150 years earlier.

All of the above is the finding out in real life instead of the indirect way of being told about it by a teacher in a classroom. This project can run for years as more is discovered, different outcomes are required (a play, a soap opera, a presentation to local people, a film of interviews, a booklet for local archives, a 'contemporary' newspaper, a website, etc.). See extracts from a school local study www.putlearningfirst/brampton/

The Plague Disaster Project

This activity is a flexible learning project for Year 9 English classes and centres on the consequences of local or global disasters and how we would survive and cope. The project is ever-topical as the latest doom-laden news broadcasts warn us of yet another imminent catastrophe.

The activities cover National Curriculum programmes of study at Key Stage 3 in English (Speaking, Listening, Reading and Writing), and ICT (Finding Things Out, Exchanging and Sharing Information).

The activities involve researching from a range of sources, selecting and presenting information, presenting and writing in a variety of styles and evaluating what has been produced. A wide range of current links are given to different disaster-related sites.

The activities are pupil-centred and open-ended so that, with teacher approval, pupils may follow their own interests within the framework of the project.

Printed materials are available from Zigzag Education.

Plague Disaster Project www.putlearningfirst.com/plague/

Inventions and discoveries

Pupils choose an invention or a discovery. They have to research:

- the actual invention or discovery (e.g. television)
- what lead up to it (e.g. wireless, electron scanning)
- how it works
- how it is used
- who helped to invent it.

The story leading to its invention or discovery is important.

- Who found it?
- Why were they looking?
- How did they and it get there?
- When did it happen?
- What exactly did happen?
- Where did it happen?
- How did it happen?
- Who was involved?
- Why did it happen?

All this requires research, recording, comparing different information sources, evaluating evidence and presenting the findings in an appropriate way. One interesting product would be a collected file of all the class work to be kept on the shelves of the Resources Centre, building a data bank of new resources.

Newspaper Day

Already mentioned above under English, this is a collaborative activity, and can be cross-curricular, in which groups of pupils acting as editorial teams work together to agree on content, write articles, take pictures, interview individuals and put together a completed newspaper within a one-day time frame.

Newspaper Day is now an annual event run by *The Times* but it can be done very simply by creating a page of news links to international news sites, defining an editorial team and the roles they are expected to fulfil, laying out deadlines, providing templates, etc. The really adventurous will consider producing scripts and a filmed news broadcast – all based on the WebQuest format above, and following the general pattern of information literacy steps.

A common theme in all these activities is the guided freedom given to pupils outside of the conventional classroom. Time and again my evaluations of these activities have positive comments from pupils saying how much they enjoyed the activities, what a change it was to find out for themselves and to be taking responsibility for their own learning.

Decision making

Major decisions, such as selecting Year 9 options for pupils' choice of GCSE subjects, what to do when you leave school, which work placements to opt for, what A levels to take or choosing your university or college course, are important decisions which benefit from real research and a methodical approach.

These decisions, based on research, questioning, collating and evaluating can be easily and very appropriately built in to pastoral time, PHSE or careers activities. They have the enormous advantage of being real-world tasks which directly affect the pupil and can take advantage of pastoral tutorial time as well as curriculum time.

Short fillers

Research and information handling doesn't have to take a great deal of time and doesn't always require extensive banks of data. Try planning *a shopping trip* (why, where to, who with, how to get there, how much do I have, how long will it take to save, how will I know when I find the right thing, etc.) or repairing a bike puncture (do I have the equipment, time and space, do I have the expertise and instructions, how do I find the puncture, how do I test that the repair is successful, etc.).

Planned designs

Try designing a new school website – or a new school. Ask people what they want, what they think of the existing situation, what they wouldn't like – and why. Record the existing situation so you can compare it with the new version and evaluate your success.

Research other examples and note the pros and cons using a SWOT analysis as in Appendix 5. Investigate costs, compile a list of features it must have, plus a wish list (ranking in order of preferences and priority). Show your plans to a range of people and incorporate their views into the final product. How successful have you been?

Problem-based learning

Problem-based learning (PBL) requires pupils to work cooperatively in groups in order to seek solutions to real-world problems. It encourages pupils 'to learn how to learn' and 'to learn how to think'. There are some sample PBL problems on the University of Delaware website at www.udel.edu/pbl/ including several group exercises that deal with everything from household wiring to a case-study problem in molecular evolution. However almost any problem posed can generate learning. Instead of the teacher giving the answer the teacher acts as mentor and facilitator, guiding pupils through the finding out process.

If you want to emphasize philosophical attitudes then the problems posed could be more open-ended, drawing on personal philosophy, but in this case problems that can be resolved by using information from accessible sources provide the task with a real purpose. In the course of finding the answer to this problem we use existing skills and knowledge, access additional information and direct it all towards resolving the problem. For example:

- Choose the right car for a family of five who like camping in summer and which would be used for the school run throughout the year. Economy and safety are very important and there must be room to carry all the family and their camping gear.
- Choose the best audio player. It should be able to play tunes downloaded from online sources and act as a sound system for parties, all for under £100. Be clear about what 'best' might mean to different consumers.
- Plan an extension to your house designed to be used as a teenage study/relaxing room. Specify appliances and check local building regulations.
- Design a water collection and storage system for your house. Specify where and how the water will be stored, whether 'grey-water waste' will be filtered, and how, including how the water could be pumped or piped to where it is most needed.

Orienteering

Orienteering is an activity which combines map reading, physical activity and problem solving. In this version the normal control posts contain a problem to be solved. This sort of problem-solving orienteering can take place within the school grounds or in a more adventurous environment. All you need is a set of maps for the building and grounds and a dozen or so problems to solve or questions to answer. Pupils work in pairs or small teams, follow a route on their map and solve the problems, which might be simple answers relating to what they see around them or might require them to find an example of something to bring back, but will probably not require them to go far from the defined route. Ideally the answers will combine to create a complete picture.

Problems arising from too many pupils following the same route can be solved either by providing several alternative routes or by having staggered starts, with the later groups occupied on a timed task (you have six minutes to list as many words starting with 'sn' as you can) before they set off, and the earlier groups doing the same task after finishing. Marks could be given for the number of control points visited, the number of correct answers given and the time taken overall. So marks will be for a combination of physical and mental activity.

A Museum of Pop Music

Design and choose exhibits for a museum of popular music. Decide what periods of music you are going to include and whether or not you will include artifacts and videos. How will you broadcast the music? Will you let people choose their preferences? Which stories will you tell and how will you tell them? 'The History of the Blues', 'The Summer of Love', 'Punk and Politics', 'the iPod generation', etc. It is very important that the facts are right and that the music matches the stories and the exhibits. Discuss how you will cope with the broadcasting of copyright songs and the publishing of copyright words and lyrics.

3
THE 20 MAIN SKILLS OF INFORMATION LITERACY

All these skills are each worth teaching on their own, but together they make up a powerful and thorough information curriculum. The order is only approximate because you may need to move rapidly back and forth between strategies depending on the precise task. Nor is the list a straight line, as evaluation may lead to a redefining of the task and new questions having to be asked.

I believe all of these skills are essential life skills. In the next chapter we shall see how 20 skills can be made into a more manageable pupil method, but these 20 skills form the backbone of any information-based activity.

They are also recognized skills within the curriculum. After each heading are alternative words describing each skill. This terminology can vary depending on the conventional language for that subject and whether this is a question-based or problem-solving activity. Following that, where appropriate, are the questions expressed as a Nine Step Plan in *School Libraries: The Foundations of the Curriculum* (1984), better known as the LISC Report. The Nine Step Plan is a series of stages a researcher should go through from asking a question through searching for answers to evaluating the task. While not the only set of methodical stages this one does seem very well reasoned and has strongly influenced this book. There is a description of the skill, examples of the skill in a curriculum context, followed by practical teaching suggestions and a web link to a relevant source of further information.

The Appendices include some related worksheets, tables and graphical organizers.

1 Questions
2 Defining the task
3 Making decisions
4 Brainstorming
5 Problem solving
6 Identifying sources
7 Locating sources
8 Selecting sources
9 Finding information within sources

10 Reading for meaning
11 Skimming and scanning
12 Evaluating material
13 Note-making
14 Sorting and arranging
15 Developing ideas
16 Presenting findings
17 Writing clearly
18 Rhetoric
19 Citing sources
20 Evaluation and review.

20 main skills of information literacy

Title	Alternative descriptions
Questions	Ask, enquire, formulate questions What do I need to do? 'Education is about learning to ask better questions'
Defining the task	Be systematic, investigate, define criteria and targets What do I need to do? Where could I go?
Making decisions	How to do this, where to start, who to work with, skills or equipment required
Brainstorming	Showering ideas, creative thinking, collective thinking, pushing the envelope, looking up and beyond, opening the mind
Problem solving	Critical thinking, SWOT analysis, identifying barriers, finding solutions, breaking down into parts
Identifying sources	Searching

	Where could I go?
	Who and what could help?
Locating sources	Find appropriate evidence
	How do I get to the information?
	What is available?
Selecting sources	Select, collect, identify relevant sources
	Which resources shall I use?
Finding information within sources	Refine search methods, interrogate sources
	How shall I use the resources?
Reading for meaning	Interpret, interrogate, understand, comprehend
Skimming and scanning	Speed-reading, understanding, comprehension
Evaluating material	Weighing arguments, triangulating sources, verifying, checking author-ship and credibility
	Examine, select and reject
Note-making	Summarize, record
	What should I make a record of and in what format?
Sorting and arranging	Repurpose, reorganize, synthesize, use graphical organizers
	Have I got the information I need?
Developing ideas	Develop, adapt, create
Presenting findings	Present, use appropriate ICT skills, use multimedia, interpret, communicate graphically and linguistically
	How should I present it?
	Who is the audience and what is their preferred method?

Writing clearly	Communicate graphically and linguistically, summarizing, précis, accuracy in a concise form
Rhetoric	Communicate effectively, convincingly and persuasively How should I present it?
Citing sources	Acknowledging sources, referencing, avoiding plagiarism, enabling information retrieval What should I make a record of? How should I present that record?
Evaluation and review	Evaluate, modify, adapt, draw conclusions What have I achieved? How might I do it better next time?

Questions

Synonyms Ask, enquire

Nine Steps What do I need to do?

Description 'Education is about learning to ask better questions.' The question we choose is likely to affect the answer we get. That's fairly obvious, yet frequently overlooked.

'Why do you hate Bob?' assumes you do hate Bob, which may not in fact be the case. Changing that assumption should change the question.

'Why is my email not working?' refers to a single symptom from what may be a more extensive issue with hardware, software or training of which broken email is only a single small consequence. The question seems to lead us into a narrow area while an effective problem solver would look at the broader picture first and try to eliminate some possible faults before zooming in on the most likely area.

'Have you got a book on hamsters?' may in fact be a request for resources on hibernation, satisfied by a video of bears rather than a book on hamsters. Of course the literal answer to this question must be either yes or no, but we should assume the questioner means *'Please find me a book about hamsters'*.

There are questions we can't easily answer. *'What's your favourite flower?'* is a matter of opinion rather than fact so the answer is not absolute. *'What's the best flower?'* will depend on what is meant by 'best'. Is it best for large displays or small posies, best for longevity, best meaning most popular?

There are closed and open questions, which have different intentions.

'Who won the FA Cup in 1951?' is a closed question – there is only one answer, that's it. (Newcastle United won 2-0 against Blackpool.)

However *'What might be the consequences of continuing to burn fossil fuels?'* is an open-ended question with a wide variety of answers, both fact and opinion.

So we need to frame our questions carefully and probably have someone else check them over first. Questionnaires by pupils frequently include unanswerable or ambiguous questions which should have been checked with a small sample of users first.

We should also recognize that while we may have a primary question, this in turn may lead to secondary and further questions, and this is a sense of enquiry we would like to encourage. Of course these additional questions deserve answers, but it may be simpler to focus on answering one question at a time, then looping back to attempt the others.

Curriculum example Getting pupils to design their own flow diagrams for questions could be helpful. This fits in with ICT aims and encourages logical and critical thinking. It also appeals to visual learners.

Asking questions about processes and materials fits in with science and design and technology, 'the interplay between empirical questions, evidence and scientific explanations ...'. Most disciplines require pupils to 'ask appropriate questions' and 'discuss and question critically'.

Teaching tip Make it a rule never to say 'Find out everything you can about . . .'. This is a thoughtless and unachievable task which leads to poor learning.

One way to explore questions in class is to use *The Black Attaché Case.*

This was a technique used by Frank Miceli to introduce questioning techniques to his pupils.

Ask pupils to think about questions which they think are worth answering. Bring in a black bag and tell the pupils you have a special computer capable of answering any question anyone asks of it. Get the class to make a list of a wide variety of questions, then say that the computer is expensive to operate and that it would be wasteful to use it for answers we already know.

The class now looks at the list and eliminates those questions where the answers are easily discovered. (How old am I?, When is my brother's birthday?, etc.) Next, say the computer has difficulty with questions which are worded vaguely or imprecisely. For example in the question '*How much information is there in the world?*' what do we mean by information, how do we count it, when do we start and stop counting, etc? Your pupils will soon realize the computer is not magic, but will also realize that analysing questions is a worthwhile task.

Miceli's pupils devised their own set of Questions about Questions which helped someone to know:

- what he was talking about
- what sort of information he wanted
- whether or not a question can be answered
- what we must do to find an answer if there is one.

Asking pupils to devise a set of rules for how to frame a question would be a very valuable exercise.

Playing a game of 'What am I thinking of?' is another way of looking at questions. The person who is 'it' thinks of something (and writes it down so they can't change their mind) then can only answer 'yes' or 'no' to all the questions the class asks. Well-targeted questions lead to fewer question steps. Try bird identification. Show some pictures of birds and ask about size, whether it's fat or short, whether the bill is curved or straight, whether the tail or wings are forked or curved, what colour it is, etc. By asking enough of these questions it is possible to identify the bird.

A prompt using the 'Wh' question words, who, what, why, where, when and how, would include simple example questions:

Who	. . . did it . . . do I ask . . . can I compare with . . . would be an expert on this . . .
What	. . . do I do next . . . is the question or task . . . do I need to find out
Why	. . . did this happen . . . does it say that . . .
Where	. . . can I find . . . do I have to go . . . do I go next
When	. . . can we start . . . does this have to done by . . . is this available
How	. . . do I get . . . do I use . . . do I make . . . can I get to . . .

Link Read the short article at
www.wildbirds.com/identify_quick.htm
See also Appendices 2 and 3.

Defining the task

Synonyms Be systematic, investigate, define criteria and targets

Nine Steps What do I need to do? Where could I go?

Description If you are looking at a task rather than directly answering a question, defining that task is essential. We need to know what we have to do and what kind of product is needed before we start. Defining the task is very important to avoid going off on a wild goose chase and producing an answer to something else entirely. Even when the purpose is to be creative and come up with wide-ranging off-the-wall solutions, it's essential to define the task at the outset. Aim to head off the dreaded phrase, 'What am I supposed to do?'

Curriculum example Defining the task applies to every curriculum subject. However the emphasis needs to be on the pupil at least as much as the teacher. Pupils checking and defining their own tasks (within strict parameters) are learning to take responsibility for their own learning.

Mathematics data handling: 'specify the problem'.

Physical education: 'use principles to plan and implement strategies'.

Teaching tip Defining the task is as important for teachers setting a task as it is for pupils performing it. Be clear about what is required in terms of:

- topic
- length (read for at least one hour, write a minimum of 250 words, etc.)
- medium (read, write, record, watch, present, etc.)
- deadline (key dates on the way, hand in no later than, etc.),
- restrictions or permissions (ask your parents to help, present it in your own handwriting, use and acknowledge at least five sources, don't copy from, etc.).

Ensuring that the task is written on the board, printed in a handout, published on the school website, accurately copied to pupils' day books, etc., helps avoid misinterpretation (I thought you meant ...). One valuable habit is to write the question or task at the top of the paper the pupil is working on – and insist they refer back to it regularly.

Another important point to make is that, as in most aspects of life, preparation is vital. Abraham Lincoln said, 'If I had eight hours to chop down a tree I'd spend six sharpening my axe'. That may be a bit extreme but it shows that preparing the ground, organizing the basics, being clear about the demands of the task, etc., will produce a better result and save time in the long run. It is very useful, for example, to discuss with pupils what are the most appropriate key words to use in searches before they start the task.

Once you have completed defining a task using the guidelines above it is useful to refer back to it to demonstrate that the framework you have used is a useful framework for pupils' own self-imposed tasks. If pupils have not defined the task they will not know whether they have achieved it.

Link Plan a Holiday www.putlearningfirst.com/holiday/step1.html

See also Appendix 4.

Making decisions

Synonyms How to do this, where to start, who to work with, skills or equipment required

Description These are decisions before you start locating sources. They may depend on the questions you are trying to answer and the task you've been given. Defining the task will help decision making, but other questions about decisions will remain.

Is this a practical way to find out or would I be better choosing somewhere closer, something simpler? Do I have enough time to complete my grand scheme or should I say, 'good enough is just good enough' and not aim too high? Can I use this equipment or that database or should I use something less powerful but which I'm familiar with? If I'm working in a group do I trust the others to complete their tasks and what do I do if they fail? Making decisions may need help, referral back to the person who set the task or an agreement on how you reach group decisions.

Curriculum example Again, decision making fits every curriculum subject providing an opportunity for pupils to take responsibility for their own learning, within the limits and alternatives set by the teacher. For example, design and technology will require pupils to 'select and use tools, equipment and processes ...'.

Teaching tip The task 'Find out about your local area' requires you to define 'local area' first. Is it your street, your town or your county? How do you decide? Is one more practical (time needed, travel requirements, people you know) than another? Take a broad task like this as an example and together with the pupils define and refine the task by making practical decisions.

'Design a suitable costume for this character' might require decisions over whether to draw or create the clothes, full size or model, using gouache, computer Paint program or fabric.

A good start for decision making is a general check list (see also Appendix 3):

- who
- what
- why
- where
- when
- how

to each of which we could add:

- is ...
- did ...
- can ...
- would ...
- will ...
- might ...

so – who is ... who did ... who can ... etc., and what is ... what did ... etc.

A teaching situation can be teacher led or pupil led. You can tell pupils what they must do, or give them the opportunity to make some kind of choice. An either/or choice gives pupils the feeling of having some control over what is happening to them while a more open choice (though not complete freedom!) gives them an opportunity to make decisions and a feeling that they are participating in their own learning. A light-hearted opening activity for this would be reading *Would You Rather?* by John Burningham (1978). More serious and practical activities could focus on examination course choices and careers, where dropping a subject at an early stage could make some career choices impossible.

Link Children Decide: Power and Participation in the Classroom
www.cfbt.com/evidenceforeducation/default.aspx?page=316

Brainstorming

Synonyms Showering ideas, creative thinking, collective thinking, pushing the envelope, looking up and beyond, opening the mind

Description This is a preparatory stage of generating ideas. Ideas about how to solve the problem, where to find solutions, who to use to help us, etc.

Brainstorming is best done in a group and has three main parts – fact finding, idea generation and solution finding. Here we concentrate on idea generation, but it is clear that before we generate ideas we need to have identified a problem, and the ideas themselves only have purpose if they are used in relation to a defined task to solve the problem.

Curriculum example Brainstorming is an ideal activity for an English or drama lesson leading to a presentation on an issue of topical interest, a 'Town meeting' for a proposed bypass or a proposal to build on the green belt. Contentious issues such as animal experimentation, meat or vegetarian diets, school uniform, NIMBY issues, etc. can all benefit from brainstorming.

Teaching tip You may need to break the problem down into smaller and more manageable chunks. It is helpful to appoint a leader at this point as well as to gently direct the minds of the group back on task. A secretary is helpful to record the ideas, though a scribble-board used by the group members can do as well or better as it encourages active participation. Criticism and scorn are forbidden.

One idea is to start with the six question words and ask who, what, how, where, when and how. Encourage pupils to open their minds and be creative. Outlandish ideas created by 'thinking outside the box' can turn into ingenious practical solutions.

Go for quantity not quality. Now is not the time to weigh up the merits of ideas, just let them come in their droves! After a while encourage the group to combine ideas as well as thinking up new ones. Half an hour is usually enough for an active brainstorming session.

Noting down your ideas using graphical organizers such as the free Mind Mapping software Freemind or simply on a board or a large piece of paper can help to create the connections which stimulate an effective brainstorming session. A blank sheet is the best worksheet for brainstorming.

Link Freemind http://freemind.sourceforge.net/wiki/index.php/Main_Page

Problem solving

Synonyms Critical thinking, identifying barriers, finding solutions

Description All information literacy is a kind of problem solving. It's finding a solution to the problem of having too much information, how to sort it out and how to make use of it.

To solve that problem we may need to ask the right questions, brainstorm possible solutions, research existing solutions and present our findings. Critical thinking is a more complex notion than can be dealt with here, but it has overlaps with problem solving in many ways.

One route through problem solving is the SWOT analysis, which works as well for personal problem solving as it does for business. List your ideas under four headings: Strengths, Weaknesses, Opportunities and Threats (see Appendix 5). Then reflect on how strengths can counteract weaknesses, how threats can be overcome and how you can make the best use of available opportunities. Breaking down what may seem an intractable problem into these four categories can start to make some sense of it and suggest some positive avenues of development.

Curriculum example Problem solving works well for careers choices and PSHE where pupils are directly affected by personal decisions.

Mathematics aims include 'select and combine known facts and problem solving strategies and resources to solve complex problems' and 'identify what further information is needed to solve a problem'.

ICT aims to 'solve problems and derive new information'.

Physical education also aims to 'use a range of problem-solving skills and techniques'.

Teaching tip Science lessons can approach problem solving by starting with brainstorming, leading to the investigation of possible solutions. A scientific investigation should look at a range of possibilities, research existing situations and solutions and propose a number of routes based on evidence.

Instead of providing pupils with a ready-made solution a science lesson aimed at problem solving could offer a variety of equipment and require pupils to devise their own method of solving a problem most effectively. How do we find out what this object is made of? Do we solve an energy crisis by reducing energy use, unearthing more fossil fuels, recycling existing materials, growing biofuels or creating microorganisms that gobble up excess carbon dioxide and convert it into useful fuels?

Su Doku puzzles provide mathematical and logical practice as does the Knight's tour (covering the chessboard as a knight moves and touching every square only once, or the ancient Tangram). In an English or drama lesson, debating a problem such as 'Where shall we put the proposed new road?' and looking at the consequences of various routes in a classroom 'council meeting' enables points of view to be expressed and solutions offered.

In geography, guiding the planners through the consequences of an out-of-town supermarket on traffic, the environment and small local shops enables pupils to explore the problem using available evidence.

Link Critical Thinking http://falcon.jmu.edu/~ramseyil/critical.htm

See also Appendix 5.

Identifying sources

Synonyms Searching

Nine Steps Where could I go? Who and what could help?

Description Information sources will vary according to the question, but a general list will include:

- people (teachers, family, experts, local politicians)
- places (library, internet, public buildings such as careers office, Citizen's Advice Bureau, archives, local records offices)
- information stores (databases, online and CD-ROM encyclo-pedias, archives, museums, dictionaries, atlases, catalogues)
- media (books, websites, databases, television, films/videos, CD-ROMs, DVDs).

Each source has its own strengths and weaknesses and again these vary depending on the particular question or task. It is helpful to identify these at an early stage. Point out, for example, that people can provide very rich and responsive details from personal experience but they are likely to be fallible in memory and bias, while databases may have bare factual detail but lack colour and character. Researching a family tree, for example, might combine personal memories of knowing great grandpa with official records of army service and census information of precisely where he lived and with whom. Comparing and contrasting different information sources can give the richest mix of fact and character.

It's worth pointing out the differences between original data and online sources. While online sources are constantly improving, there are advantages in visiting the original. Though secondary sources may be more easily accessed they can also be edited and may omit key data. A scribbled marginal note may provide you with more crucial information than the main text itself. Watching a kestrel hunting over a field of wild flowers offers more than an illustration on a website.

Curriculum example Every curriculum subject should offer opportunities for finding out, using a range of resources for accessing information. Using information skills will make the most of the opportunity. English teachers will aim to 'select, compare and synthesise information from different texts'; history, modern foreign languages and geography teachers will 'identify, select and use a range of appropriate sources of information';

Science teachers will consider 'whether to use evidence from first-hand experience or secondary sources'.

Teaching tip Set up an example where pupils can *only* go to one of the four types of resources. What are they missing by being restricted in their choice? What problems would they have in using only one?

Provide a list of all the information sources given above and discuss which would be the best and which the worst for a given task (e.g. World War I history, whereabouts of historic roads and tracks, train times and up-to-date arrival times, star patterns for next month, the effect on people of a particular disaster, etc.).

Link Plan a Holiday www.putlearningfirst.com/holiday/step3.html
See also Appendix 6.

Locating sources

Synonyms Find appropriate evidence

Nine Steps How do I get to the information? What is available?

Description Online access is unlikely to be a problem, with free internet at school, libraries and, often, at home, but access to distant libraries and museums, rare archived material, etc., may only be practical via the internet or via catalogues and guide books.

A good library/Resources Centre should have a wide range of resources in terms of content and medium. It should also have links to further, more detailed or more specialized knowledge, even if it doesn't hold it on site.

Catalogues and museum CDs will lead on to the museum or

gallery itself; phone books will lead to further places and people who may have specialized knowledge.

The Resources Centre should hold CDs, audio and video tapes, DVDs, fiction and non-fiction books, ephemera such as leaflets and handouts, clippings from newspapers, internet access and, where possible, realia or access to it. A good resources catalogue will give not only title, author, publisher and Dewey catalogue number, but what medium the information is stored on and, where appropriate, a picture of it and an indication of where it is stored.

A child wanting information about badgers should be able to choose from *The Child's Book of Mammals*, the Badger Trust website (at www.badger.org.uk/) a stuffed badger, a film of badgers in the wild, maps where they can be found and details of wildlife centres where they can be seen in natural conditions, including those with live webcams.

Curriculum example In all these cases, in all curriculum areas, pupils will use information sources to identify further information sources – the perfect task for the library/Resources Centre.

Teaching tip Oral history collections and personally visiting and interviewing local people will be helpful for biographies, local history and geography projects as well as community relations.

Maps and atlases will help identify useful places; town maps are best for local buildings; Ordnance Survey maps for rural areas and landscape features; atlases for more distant spots; census returns to identify a particular place at a particular time in history.

Phone books and websites can lead to useful and helpful people, as long as pupils are clear about what to ask and understand what it is appropriate to ask and who has no obligation to answer. Collections in libraries and archives in local records offices often house directories and catalogues that can link several different information sources – matching the census to a trade directory and to an old OS map.

Activities such as matching a list of topics to a range of sources are useful here. A resource-based quiz requiring a wide range of different media and resource types would demonstrate the breadth of stock available in the library/Resources Centre.

Selecting sources

Synonyms Select, collect, identify relevant sources

Nine Steps Which resources shall I use?

Description Here we come back to the primary question: Does the information you've found help answer the question? If not, leave it out. There is, however, every reason to make a note of where information is held so you can come back to it (record addresses, phone numbers, website URLs, Dewey numbers, titles and authors of books), even if you don't read them.

Curriculum example ICT is one of many subjects requiring pupils to, 'select appropriate resources'. History and geography projects require pupils to compare a range of primary and secondary information sources and English curricula require pupils to 'select, compare, synthesise and sift'.

Mathematics aims to 'select and combine known facts', 'select and organise appropriate resources' while design and technology aims to 'identify relevant sources of information'. Science deals with ideas and evidence.

Teaching tip Simply setting a limit – both maximum and minimum – on the number of resources helps focus pupils' minds on the task. They inevitably become more selective when they can only choose three resources.

Better still, stipulate a minimum number of resources are to be used in total, a maximum to be collected at any one time and that the range of resources must include at least one book, one online source and one person. Vary this depending on your situation, so that there are enough good-quality resources to go round the class, enough terminals through which to access the internet and a need to find a person and credible source in school, locally or at home.

These limits force pupils to think about worthwhile sources and to prioritize them. It is especially useful to get pupils to explain and justify their choice.

This is also an opportunity to consider the thoughtful use of search engines, phrasing searches to narrow down the number of potential sources instead of relying upon Google rankings. A very worthwhile lesson can be spent comparing three or four web pages of resources on a common theme. What criteria do we use to decide which source is useful and which is not?

Consider relevance, topicality, authenticity, authorship, appropriateness of language, readability, thoroughness and detail, etc.

Link Plan a Holiday www.putlearningfirst.com/holiday/step3.html
See also Appendix 7.

Finding information within sources

Synonyms Refine search methods, interrogate sources

Nine Steps How shall I use the resources?

Description First we must return to the original task or the primary question. With this in mind and possibly after a few preliminary searches, we should have a number of key words to help our search. Key words used in certain combinations (see Chapter 7 for more detail) can turn up useful online and electronic sources which may in turn lead to useful answers. Key words are also useful for scanning book chapter headings and searching in indexes.

Familiarity with alphabetical order – and not simply the first letter of a word – is very important, as is an understanding of the conventions of the index, contents pages and bold headwords in dictionaries.

Curriculum example Design and technology will require pupils to 'identify relevant sources of information' while history may express it as 'identify, select and use a range of appropriate sources'. Modern foreign languages emphasizes 'how to use dictionaries and other reference materials appropriately and effectively' while in English students will 'sift, summarise and use the most important points' as well as 'extract meaning beyond the literal'.

Teaching tip Always urge pupils to go back to the primary question and ruthlessly put aside anything which does not answer that question. If a note of the source of such extra information is kept then nothing is lost. Electronic searches often lead to more information than is manageable and the temptation to mindlessly copy and paste does nothing to discriminate between the worthy and the worthless.

One teaching technique is to ban copy and paste for a while and make pupils write notes by hand. This encourages brevity and selection.

Different techniques may be used for different media – use of indexes comparing the contents of several different books, some specialist, some general; using different search engines, different search terms and comparing results.

The basic skills of using alphabetical order are vital, so have regular exercises of arranging words in alphabetical order, making sure that this goes further than the first letter of a word.

Similarly, understanding the difference between the contents pages and the index, the way that headwords are arranged in an index, the use of headings and subheadings to arrange material in an orderly way and the way dictionaries and encyclopedias use headers and footers to feature the first and last words on a page, are essential book skills.

Speed searching competitions are good lesson starters. See also 'Evaluating' and 'Note-making' below.

Link Search engines www.putlearningfirst.com/holiday/tips/tips3.html

Reading for meaning

Synonyms Interpret, interrogate, understand, comprehend

Description This is a language skill, traditionally called comprehension. The difference in this situation, however, is that the questions which pupils use to interrogate the text are compiled by the pupils themselves. This rather adds to the difficulty level, though it makes it a far more real-life task.

Curriculum example English teachers could ring the changes on traditional comprehension exercises by providing the text but asking pupils to write their own questions (and answers). This is a useful exercise from several points of view and is a valuable challenge. Interpretation of events and data is so hedged around by different cultural and historic issues that there is no shortage of material to look at.

English students will 'sift, summarise and use the most important points' ... 'to extract meaning beyond the literal'.

Modern foreign languages students will be 'listening, reading or viewing for personal interest and enjoyment as well as for information'.

Teaching tip The exercise above can be turned into a class discussion on meaningful questions and interpreting texts. Interpretation issues become more interesting when there are several heads with differing points of view.

English literature, history source material and science data are all full of examples of information which is open to interpretation.

Arrange a class discussion on a contentious issue and focus on a single piece of ambiguous data before pitting pupils against each other. There are examples to start you off in Chapter 2, but a simple interpretation could be as immediate as 'I saw you chatting up my girlfriend', versus 'I was only talking about the weather'.

SQ3R is a five-stage, active reading technique for making the most of reading time. It helps to organize the structure of a subject in the reader's mind. It also helps to separate important information from irrelevant data.

The stages are:

- *Survey* – scan the contents, introduction, chapter introductions and chapter summaries to pick up an overview of the text.

- *Question* – make a note of questions that come to mind and think of them as targets to find out more about.
- *Read* – read through useful sections in detail, making sure you understand all the relevant points. Note this information for future use. Anything you don't understand but which might prove useful becomes a question (above).
- *Recall* – go through the key information in your mind and make sure you know how it links together.
- *Review* – a final run through. This could be useful revision after a short space of time has elapsed, or your understanding could best be reviewed by explaining it to someone else.

Skimming and scanning

Synonyms Speed reading, understanding, comprehension

Description Skimming is used to obtain the overall sense of a text, for example to assess whether it's relevant and useful to read in more detail. Scanning is used to hunt for particular information from a text, for example to find a name in a telephone directory.

These techniques for effective reading are part of the English and modern foreign languages curricula and include ICT-based sources. Many modern jobs require reading through a large quantity of information searching for relevant points, so skimming and scanning are immensely practical and time-saving skills which deserve to be taught rather than caught.

Young children start to read by looking at each letter, then move on to a word at a time. Most effective readers look at blocks of text of varying sizes, with speed increasing as the size of the block taken in at one glance increases. However we frequently glance back at previous blocks or on to future blocks, which makes comprehension more difficult.

Speed reading uses both skimming and scanning and aims to improve reading skills by:

- increasing the number of words read in each block

- reducing the length of time spent reading each block
- reducing the number of times your eyes skip back to a previous sentence.

Some people find they can slide their eyes down the centre of a page taking in the general meaning of the words on either side using peripheral vision.

Curriculum example English students will aim to 'sift, summarise and use the most important points' while modern foreign languages teachers may show 'techniques for skimming and for scanning written texts for information'.

Teaching tip Tips for skimming:

1. Read title, subtitles and subheading to find out what the text is about.
2. Look at the illustrations too.
3. Read the first and last sentence of each paragraph and/or the first and last paragraph of a longer piece.
4. Don't read every word or every sentence. Let your eyes skim over the text, taking in key words.

Tips for scanning:

1. Concentrate on what you're looking for but let your eyes roam.
2. Don't try to read every word. Let your eyes scan quickly across the page.
3. Use headings and titles to guide you.
4. In a dictionary or phone book, use header words at the top of each page to guide you.
5. Use alphabetical order to guide you through catalogues and dictionaries.

Practise skimming on any page of text. A textbook, newspaper or encyclopedia article are ideal. Give pupils a very short time to skim the whole page then get them to answer simple questions on the content from anywhere in the text.

Practise scanning by looking up a given recipe in a cookbook index, a name in a newspaper, a taxi in Yellow Pages or an unusual name in the phone book, or scan web pages on the internet for specific information. Aim for speed and basic retrieval, not detail. Timed races are competitive and fun. Vary the layout and reading level of the text as well as the time allowed.

Another variation, which is not really reading at all, is to glance for a second at a picture and attempt to remember all the information the picture presents. It becomes clear that very little time is needed to absorb a large amount of information. It is for this reason that 'flash frames' – single advertising film frames flashed onto the screen during broadcasts – have been banned. The flashed message may be taking unfair advantage of the viewer's unconscious mind.

Link Skimming www.bbc.co.uk/skillswise/words/reading/techniques/skimming/index.shtml

Scanning www.bbc.co.uk/skillswise/words/reading/techniques/scanning/index.shtml

Speed reading www.mindtools.com/pages/article/newISS_03.htm

Evaluating material

Synonyms Weighing arguments, triangulating sources, verifying, checking authorship and credibility

Nine Steps Examine, select and reject

Description Evaluating resources and sources of information requires intelligence and an understanding of the subject, but can be helped by a simple checklist.

A class could compile a list of information which is reliable and which is dubious depending on:

- its date

- whether it's edited and published by a well-known publisher or an individual author
- printed or a website
- the author's reputation and qualifications
- any known bias by association with known organizations
- internal factual contradictions
- contrast with other known sources
- origin
- web address
- internal evidence such as factual errors, spelling and grammar faults, etc.

Evaluating material has been summarized more formally as Authority, Accuracy, Objectivity, Currency and Usability. It was memorably expressed by John Dewey: 'We can have facts without thinking but we cannot have thinking without facts' (www.quotatiospage.com/quote/32951.html).

It's worth noting that Wikipedia itself, though a wonderful source of information from a wide swathe of contributors, does not claim to be a definitive source of information:

> not everything in Wikipedia is accurate, comprehensive, or unbiased. Many of the general rules of thumb for conducting research apply to Wikipedia, including:
> - Always be wary of any one single source (in any medium – web, print, television or radio), or of multiple works that derive from a single source.
> - Where articles have references to external sources (whether online or not) read the references and check whether they really do support what the article says.
> - In all academic institutions, Wikipedia, along with most encyclopaedias, is unacceptable as a major source for a research paper.
> (http://en.wikipedia.org/wiki/Wikipedia:Researching_with_Wikipedia)

Wikipedia recognizes that its strengths are in its broad base of contributors but that the downside is that it is not authoritative

77

and is vulnerable to unevenness of quality 'since individual articles will, by their nature, vary in standard and maturity'.

I recommend a visit to the Wiki Scanner at wikiscanner.virgil.gr/ which reveals self-interested edits made by people who change Wikipedia entries to show themselves in a more favourable light. Start by reading 'Wired's list of salacious edits'.

Curriculum example History projects require you to compare primary and secondary information sources while English students should 'take different views into account' and geographers will 'analyse and evaluate evidence'.

Teaching tip When the police take a statement they check what they've been told against other known facts. If they find that the facts which they can check are true, they may tend to believe the rest of your story – even if they can't prove it. The same is true of information. Let's say you are researching global warming and find two sources of information. If you can prove you are a professor of climatology at a university, using the university website to store your pages and you write formally with references to other sources, you may be a credible source. But if you have a Hotmail address, misspell your work and can't prove you are who you are, you may be less credible. Although if you've just survived a hurricane, your first-hand account may have the edge.

In a courtroom the police, having made their own investigations, must present their evidence to the court, while other evidence and interpretation is made by the counsel for the defence. A judge and jury must then evaluate the evidence and decide. Pupils have to do the same thing, if in less stressful circumstances. A role play of a courtroom deciding on evidence would be a good scenario for a class looking at evaluating sources.

The class can compile their own set of reliable and unreliable sources for a given topic, perhaps with a star rating plus justification for their decisions.

Link Strengths and weaknesses of resources www.putlearningfirst.com/holiday/tasks/tasks41.html

Accuracy and reliability
www.putlearningfirst.com/holiday/tips/tips4.html

Web hoaxes
http://hoaxbusters.ciac.org/

The good, the bad and the ugly http://lib.nmsu.edu/instruction/
eval.html

See also Appendix 8.

Note-making

Synonyms Summarize, record

Nine Steps What should I make a record of and in what format?

Description The first priority is to be clear about the primary
question. What are you trying to answer? Does this information
help? If so, note it down; if not, leave it out – but make a note
elsewhere so you can find it again if necessary.

The second priority is to develop a quick and effective note-
making technique which can keep up with the flow of information,
be compact but be able to include the essence of the original and be
able to recreate the significant content from it. Good notes should
be like condensed soup – the essential bits are concentrated into a
small space and you can recreate the whole quite simply.

Curriculum example Art and design students need to 'record and
analyse first hand observations' while in mathematics students
aim to 'collect data from a variety of suitable sources'. History
students will 'select and record information relevant to the
enquiry' and in geography students 'collect, record and present
evidence'. Science students must make thorough notes on their
observations and experiments.

Teaching tip The tendency to copy everything electronically is
understandable but the result is too much undigested clutter.
Best practice may be to start by writing notes by hand, using

abbreviations, getting facts and details down but leaving out extra description and unnecessary detail. Alternatively a word processing outliner can provide an overall structure which is filled in as more findings are made.

Aim for key words – the words which have the most significance and the most relevant sense in the shortest possible way.

When you read an information source and find something which could be useful, note it down. Include where you found it and who wrote it. (See how to acknowledge sources, below.)

Some learners prefer lists with subheadings and bullet points, others prefer pictures and graphics, others again prefer mind maps, tables, charts and similar graphic organizers. What is best depends on the preferred learning style and the nature of the topic. It's important that learners have the opportunity to experiment and find out their favourite and most effective style.

One trick is the Trash or Treasure technique. Tell your pupils that they are looking for the most important words – the treasure – and they'll be able to bin the unnecessary words – the trash. Take a page from an encyclopedia and copy it onto a slide. Read it aloud to the class and then say you are going on a treasure hunt together. Discuss which words can be 'trashed' without spoiling the original meaning and cross these out, leaving only the 'treasure'.

Now ask the pupils to retell the passage in their own words using only the treasure words as prompts.

To apply this to their research, give each pupil a photocopy of a text and tell them to use a soft pencil to cross out the trash. Then transfer the treasure to a separate sheet together with a note on the source of the information.

Pupils can do this for themselves without destroying the original text either by highlighting the text using Word's highlighter or simply deleting text from a copy of the original.

Link Mind Tools
www.mindtools.com/mindmaps.html

Free Mind – free mind mapping software
http://freemind.sourceforge.net/wiki/index.php/Main_Page

Sorting and arranging

Synonyms Repurpose, reorganize, synthesize

Nine Steps Have I got the information I need?

Description The process of note-taking and referring back to the primary question should have thrown up useful key words and topic headings which can be used to organize the topic. However organizing material is different from organizing an essay or presentation. Just as collating evidence from a crime scene could lead to a journalist summarizing the findings in the first paragraph but a thriller writer keeping it to the very end, organization of raw material may follow a different pattern from the organization of an essay. Sometimes a database or spread-sheet is a better data gatherer than the word processor or presentation tool used to deliver the end product.

It may be useful to create a formal list of headings and subheadings, thinking in terms of chapters and paragraphs. Even a report written in continuous prose will benefit from draft headings and subheadings, which can be removed later if required. Subheadings can be used as a framework to link to slides in a presentation.

A web processing outliner such as the one built in to Microsoft Word can help in structuring a piece of writing, emphasizing headings and hiding content when necessary. A writing program such as Scrivener, (www.literatureandlatte.com/scrivener.html) described as 'The word processor with a cork board' will help organization and work flow and the browser plug-in Zotero (www.zotero.org/) is a free easy-to-use Firefox extension to help you collect, manage and cite your research sources. Any word processor will help rearrange, edit and organize lists, ideas and words.

Curriculum example Most curriculum subjects, including art and design and English, will seek to 'organize and present ideas and information in different ways'. English may specifically aim to 'use a range of techniques and different ways of organising and structuring material to convey ideas, themes and characters'. A good practical exercise in sorting and arranging information is to compile a CV for a job, in preparation for a careers event or a work placement.

Teaching tip Start by providing a set of headings and subheadings as scaffolding for pupils' writing. The pupils add content as they go along.

A discussion or argument can be created with a simple two-column grid with areas for 'For', 'Against' and 'Other'.

Simply arranging facts into categories helps sort things out in your mind and this can be done using a pile of headings and a pile of paragraphs all printed on card and spread around the room. Pupils have to organize the paragraphs meaningfully under useful headings.

A table is a simple graphical way of organizing content. A mind map may be more elaborate and more effective for a more complex topic.

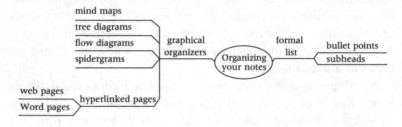

Wall posters, displays, collections of artefacts, presentations, etc. may all have different strengths in bringing together information in different combinations and juxtapositions. Often, having two unexpected items or ideas together sparks off new thoughts.

Link Free Mind – free mind mapping software
http://freemind.sourceforge.net/wiki/index.php/Main_Page

Developing ideas

Synonyms Develop, adapt, create

Description While research may start with finding out what is already known, it may also develop new and original ideas. Brainstorming and mind mapping are two skills which may encourage this, by putting existing information into unexpected combinations, making new associations and connections and in turn leading to fresh thinking.

New ideas often build on existing ideas and extend them or connect them up. They may come from unexpected associations and be rightly described as creative.

Creativity can involve working together and problem solving, stimulating the imagination, and creating events and objects. Opportunities for creative imagination can be provided and to some extent creative skills can be taught.

Curriculum example Art, drama and PE can provide the opportunities for older children which the sandbox, model-making, finger painting and play can provide for the youngest children. Most subjects can provide opportunities for the child's imagination to flow unrestrainedly. Animation software can help create new imaginative worlds.

English teachers will urge pupils to 'use imaginative vocabulary', art and design teachers to ' explore and develop ideas ' and music teachers to 'create and develop musical ideas'.

Teaching tip Restrictions and limitations can be a good thing to motivate creativity. Giving a group a problem to be solved with only limited equipment forces them to concentrate and squeeze the best ideas from a restricted area.

Examples of this include outdoor and adventurous activities such as building rafts to carry the group across a lake, or using poles and milk crates to cross a defined obstacle.

Open-ended activities include finding as many uses as you can for a brick (using unlimited imagination), writing stories which must include a list of given words or items, while drama activities including role play can break down some of the social barriers which restrict imaginative action.

The creative process has been described as a four-step plan:

- *Preparation* – research; the gathering of ideas
- *Incubation* – playing with the ideas
- *Illumination* – Eureka! I got it!
- *Validation* – test out the idea.

This may seem rather formal and codified, but it does show creativity in context, supported practically by research and evaluation. Simply juxtaposing unusual items and inviting pupils to try to see a connection can bring about creative ideas.

Link Excellence and Enjoyment (DfES 2003)
www.standards.dfes.gov.uk/primary/publications/literacy/63553/

Presenting findings

Synonyms Present, use appropriate ICT skills, use multimedia, interpret, communicate graphically and linguistically

Nine Steps How should I present it? Who is the audience and what is their preferred method?

Description Presentations can be personal, to a large or a small audience, face to face, spoken, drawn or written, music or dance, using simple or advanced ICT software and equipment, etc. The range is very wide indeed.

A good presentation is an effective communication act, aiming to inform, explain, describe or persuade. It may be well prepared or spontaneous.

The general skills of communicating successfully, whether graphically by written or the spoken word, are important to us both socially and professionally, as individuals or as part of a team. It is equally important to be able to convince your partner verbally as the traffic warden or your boss; it is important to write persuasively to get people to give you a job, to accept your excuse or to be convinced by your product proposal.

The following have been defined (Engleberg 1994) as 'the 7 Ps of Presentation' – Preparation, People, Place, Purpose, Presence, Passion and Personality. The last two elements show that presentation is not simply a technical achievement, but a means of convincing by body language and rhetoric as well as message and content.

Note also the synonym 'interpret' which describes more than simply transmitting information. Interpreting suggests communicating successfully and convincingly so the audience really understands the meaning, which in turn implies a full understanding by the speaker.

Also remember to develop 'awakening devices' in case your audience is in danger of nodding off. What is fascinating for you as you prowl around the room the centre of attention and hit with adrenaline may send some seated listeners off to sleep, especially after a good lunch. So vary the output, moving from personal delivery to slides, to activities, to audio, to prevent monotony.

For example:

- increase your voice volume
- vary your voice inflection and rhythm
- show a picture
- add movement to slides – where it's helpful
- hold up or send around a prop
- move around the room
- tell a story
- crack a simple (and appropriate) joke but don't use humour for its own sake
- write on a flip chart
- invite the audience to write on the flip chart
- arrange an activity which involves the audience moving, thinking, doing, whether solo or alone, but excepting potentially embarrassing activities, please.

Curriculum example All curriculum subjects require pupils to present ideas and information in a wide variety of ways. In English this may be 'Writing to imagine, explore or entertain, inform, explain, describe, persuade, argue advise ...'. Also to 'present material clearly, using appropriate layout, illustrations and organisation'.

Elsewhere, whether graphical techniques or ICT are specified, or a range of resources and data are referred to, we may sum up the aims as 'use a range of tools to create good quality presentations in a form that is sensitive to the needs of particular audiences and suits the information content' (*England and Wales National Curriculum for ICT at Key Stage 3*, paragraph 3c).

Teaching tip Presentation software using sounds and images, displayed on an interactive whiteboard, can be created to a high standard by teacher and pupil alike. Care needs to be taken with prepared templates and clipart which may provide gloss without content. The content and purpose of a presentation should take precedence over mere appearance and pupils should be encouraged to explain their purpose and describe their audience.

Writing original stories using presentation software can be a good avenue for creativity as well as very entertaining for the class. The Rhetoric chart below describes a way to organize a spoken presentation. One approach to encourage thinking and planning is to devise a storyboard on paper before starting the presentation software. This can encourage imagination and planning rather than having the software take over. However a good piece of presentation software provides so many transitions between slides and graphical and animated elements that these can either encourage imagination and enable the pupil's message – or overwhelm it with gimmicks to the extent of losing the core message. Wise teachers will assess which temptation their pupils are likely to succumb to and guide them elsewhere.

Link ICT Presentations
www.standards.dfes.gov.uk/schemes2/secondary_ICT/ ict02/

The 7 Ps of Presentation *(after Engleberg 1994)*

Ps	Questions	Dos and Don'ts
Preparation	Where and how can you find good ideas and information for your presentation?	Adapt existing material to new audiences and places. Use relevant topical examples.

	How much and what kind of supporting materials do you need?	
People	Who is your audience? How do the characteristics, skills, opinions and attitudes of your audience affect your purpose?	Is your language appropriate? Is your material relevant? Are you giving your audience what they want or need?
Place	Why are you speaking to this audience now and in this place? How can you plan and adapt to the logistics of this place? How can you use visual aids to help you achieve your purpose?	Arrive early. Check electrics, projector bulbs, and lighting, hide trailing leads, lay out equipment and notes. Make sure you can be seen and heard. Can your slide be read from the back of the room?
Purpose	Why are you speaking? What do you want the audience to know, think, believe or do as a result of your presentation?	Get this clear in your mind and remind yourself often. Be clear about this in your introduction.
Planning	Is there a natural order to the ideas and information you will use? What are the most effective ways to organize your presentation to adapt it to the purpose, people, place, etc.?	Organize and stick to a running order – don't go back over it except in response to questions from the floor. When you've said it, shut up!

Performance	What form of delivery is best suited to the purpose of your presentation? What delivery techniques will make your presentation more effective? How should you practise?	Don't just read from notes (though of course you can refer to them). Avoid fumbling and fidgeting (get someone to check on you beforehand while you practise).
Personality Presence Passion	How do you become associated with your message in a positive way? What can you do to demonstrate your competence, charisma and character to the audience?	Engage eye contact, talk to people individually as they come in. Smile!

Writing clearly

Synonyms Communicate graphically and linguistically, summarizing, précis, accuracy in a concise form

Description Précis was once a commonly practised skill in schools, and deserves to be again. The art of retaining the important points while discarding the unnecessary goes to the heart of information literacy and is an important business skill. Furthermore, organizing an essay, report or presentation is only partly about organizing the raw material; it is also about organizing the page into a coherent argument with meaningful paragraphs and impactful sentences. The structure of an essay need not be dictated by the pattern of its source material. For example, a history essay need not be chronological and a literary essay need not parallel the plot.

Curriculum example In English, the skills of handwriting and presentation emphasize effective and accurate communication. Exercises in describing and conveying information are always worthwhile.

Using graphic techniques and ICT to communicate is also important in design and technology, Art and any other subject such as geography or mathematics where data can best be expressed graphically rather than in words.

Teaching tip Giving advice on how much a text should be summarized or reduced is very difficult. However, reducing by a percentage – say 25 per cent or 10 per cent – could be a useful aim. The key target is to reduce the length while retaining the important content.

Using a word processor is useful, as a pupil can write something, keep this as a saved file and then delete the 'unnecessary' content to leave a précis, without rewriting the whole piece, or losing the original.

Look at 'executive summaries' of documents and reports as examples. Book 'blurbs' also reduce information and highlight key points, though they do this with the intention of persuading.

Look also at word processing tools such as Microsoft Word's AutoSummarize tool, which tries to automatically analyse a text for repeated words and phrases and come up with a précis reduced by the percentage you choose. Note that while this may work on some long documents the program does struggle with any text shorter than 5,000 words. Nevertheless, it could provide a good comparison for pupils writing their own.

Writing to a word limit is a different kind of exercise which can be linked to the work of journalists in a newspaper scenario. Provide some facts and set a word limit so a sub-editor can fit the story into the space available. Excess wordage will be ruthlessly cut. Provide a time limit too, to meet a newspaper's printing deadline.

Exercises developing effective written communication include dividing the class into teams, each of which builds a house or a castle with Lego. Each team then describes its building to another team which has to construct a copy – without looking at it. Success is rated by how close the two models are to each other.

You can do a similar exercise, Draw, Describe, Replicate, where each pupil draws a picture, describes it in writing then gives the written description to a partner who, not having seen the drawing, has to replicate it. Again the more similar the two drawings the more successful the description.

Link Summarizing
www.bbc.co.uk/skillswise/words/reading/summarising/factsheet.shtml

The Owl Writing Lab http://owl.english.purdue.edu/

Rhetoric

Synonyms Communicate effectively, convincingly and persuasively

Nine Steps How should I present it?

Description Rhetoric has got itself a bad name by being associated with a lack of truth from politicians and advertising. It is sometimes seen as seeking to persuade a worthless case. However rhetoric can be plain and persuasive, with the speaker respected and the case honestly presented. Used together with examples it can create the very best of presentations.

There are five basic Canons of Rhetoric:

- *Invention* – what is said
- *Arrangement* – how it is organized
- *Style* – the expression used to deliver it
- *Memory* – delivering from the heart and mind, not read from a script
- *Delivery* – how it is said.

The six divisions of Arrangement are:

1 *Introduction* – to put the audience in the right frame of mind, e.g. 'Friends, Romans and countrymen . . .'.
2 *Narration* – a short statement of the facts of the case.

90

3   *Division* – the main headings under which the subject will be treated.
4   *Proof* – the orator marshals all the arguments on his/her side of the case, giving points in ascending order of importance leading to a climax. This is the core of the argument.
5   *Refutation* – the orator attempts to answer or discredit the arguments advanced against him/her.
6   *Conclusion*
    a.   summing up
    b.   amplification – an emphatic statement of the speaker's position, often invoking 'commonplaces' to move the audience to indignation or enthusiasm
    c.   an appeal to the audience's tender feelings.

Curriculum example In English pupils will wish to 'use vocabulary, structures and grammar of standard spoken English fluently and accurately'. In mathematics, too, pupils will 'interpret and discuss the data'.

Teaching tip Using rhetoric to persuade can be done with or without evidence.

Presenting the results from your science experiment and attempting to persuade the class that your conclusions are correct is at least as valuable as trying to persuade the drama or English class that the line of the new bypass should or should not go past their houses.

The rules of rhetoric were devised by Socrates and Cicero, amongst others, and still apply to effective speaking today. Offer these to the class as a model before they make their own presentations.

Link The Forest of Rhetoric
http://humanities.byu.edu/rhetoric/silva.htm

Rhetoric, Language in Use
www.putlearningfirst.com/language/20rhet/20rhet.html

Getting the Buggers to Find Out

Using rhetoric to argue and persuade

Division	Purpose	Example
Introduction	to put the audience in the right frame of mind.	Welcome, friends, colleagues, students and guests ...
Narration	a short statement of the facts of the case.	We are here to congratulate the students of 2006 on their great successes to praise them and to recall some of their achievements.
Division	the main headings under which the subject will be treated.	I'd like to look at academic achievements such as examination success, sporting achievements and achievement in the arts.
Proof	the orator marshals all the arguments on his/her side of the case, giving points in ascending order of importance leading to a climax. This is the core of the argument.	Let us start with a community success, however, as we recall the very popular free concert and picnic in June ...
Refutation	the orator attempts to answer or discredit the arguments advanced against him/her.	To those who say, the college has always attracted the most brilliant students and so success comes easily, I say ...
Conclusion	a. summing up	So 2006 was a particularly successful year.

b. amplification – an emphatic statement of the speaker's position, often invoking 'commonplaces' to move the audience to indignation or enthusiasm.	Our college continues to uphold the very highest standards of behaviour and striving for the best. What else are the stars for?
c. an appeal to the audience's tender feelings.	And so to each and every one of you I can honestly say, 'I am proud to have known you. Go out into the world and tell them you were proud of this college'. Thank you.

Citing sources

Synonyms Acknowledging sources, referencing, avoiding plagiarism, enabling information retrieval

Nine Steps What should I make a record of? How should I present that record?

Description Acknowledging sources of information has two main purposes

First, the writer is recognizing that someone else did some work for them, and that while overall the work is that of the writer these parts borrowed from other sources need to be cited. Second, the sources are listed and referred to so anyone can read the original source material and make their own minds up about how to interpret it or follow up the evidence from the original. The examples in Chapter 2 show how important interpretation is.

Curriculum example History students routinely 'select and record', design and technology students 'identify relevant sources'.

Citing sources should be a compulsory aspect of any research work in order to guard against plagiarism and this is especially true when online or other digital sources are used.

It is important to emphasize that while knowledge may be free, the way it is expressed by an author is copyright, and that passing off someone else's work as your own is theft, just as much as it would be to steal his/her possessions. Plagiarism is rife in the information age and large numbers of pupils copy and paste whole pages then pass it off as their own. This has given coursework in particular a bad name. Yet there are several easy ways of preventing the most obvious kinds of plagiarism.

There are dedicated websites which can, for a fee, check pupils' work against massive databases to see if it is genuine. Teachers can do this for themselves, too, by typing in a suspicious sentence from a pupil's work and entering it into Google. If there's a match, you'll know it's not original – though actually the online example might not be original either!

Google Scholar is an excellent place to find research material with bibliographical details, suitable mainly for teacher or sixth-form research. It's a good example of how to reference research work.

Teaching tip Present the message that plagiarism is theft. Stealing someone else's work and passing it off as your own is deceitful. And while you're doing this reflect on the copyright laws when you next photocopy something.

Set up a mock piece of work on an appropriate topic and in front of the class run it through Google for matches. Don't tell them you've written it using borrowed phrases, but watch them as it dawns on them that you could do this for their work too, and find how much they have copied from others.

Equally it is worthwhile explaining that you, as a skilled teacher, can spot unevenness of style in pupils' writing and will be suspicious of unexpectedly mature writing from an average candidate. It is in the pupils' own interest that they are able to quote their sources to help show which pieces of writing are genuinely their own.

Insist on the Harvard pattern below for any academic work. Author and title are always essential; Dewey number, date and web addresses are important too.

Link The Forest of Rhetoric
http://humanities.byu.edu/rhetoric/silva.htm
Google Scholar http://scholar.google.com/

The Harvard pattern for recording your sources

Book

The details required for a book, in order, are:

1 name(s) of author/s, editor/s, compiler/s (surname, and initials or given name) or the institution responsible
2 year of publication
3 title of publication
4 series title and individual volume if any
5 edition, if other than first
6 publisher
7 place of publication
8 page number(s) if applicable.

Example

Grey, D. S., 2006. *Getting the Buggers to Learn. Continuum. London.*

Internet

The details required for an internet source, in order, are:

1 name(s) of author/s
2 date of publication
3 title of publication
4 publisher/organization
5 edition, if other than first
6 type of medium
7 date item retrieved
8 site address (URL).

Example

Grey, D. S. 2005, 'Plan a holiday with the six step plan', Put Learning First, [Online] Accessed February 2007.

Available at: www.putlearningfirst.com/holiday/

Evaluation and review

Synonyms Evaluate, modify, adapt, draw conclusions

Nine Steps What have I achieved? How might I do it better next time?

Description At this point you need to look back and take stock. You need to ask 'Have I done what I set out to do?' – and if not, go back and improve things. You need to go back to the primary question or task and check you really have answered the question. It's all too easy to get piles of answers and materials which don't actually answer the first question you were set.

Curriculum example Many subjects will require pupils to 'be clear about what they have actually achieved', or 'suggest improvements'. Many schools require pupils to review their end of term reports and certainly reflection and review of completed work, recent behaviour and events is of great value – if it is followed by action intended to improve.

A genuine evaluation is frequently asked for after an activity and although a quick-fix answer is too often, 'I would spend a bit more time on "x" but overall I am quite pleased with what I've done' a genuine response would look at every stage and ask 'Is it the best answer?' and 'How could I have done better?'.

Evaluation makes this information method a circular one, reviewing to improve at every stage, not just the final one when it is too late to change anything.

Teaching tip Help pupils identify what's good and what can be improved in their work. Be constructive rather than destructive in criticism. Then help them write down targets, using the phrases, 'How I can improve ...' or 'Next time I will ...'. Naturally this is likely to come at the end of an activity or piece of research. Nevertheless, leave time for it to be done well. If evaluation is crammed into the rushed final minutes of a lesson it will not be valued. Similarly it's important to revisit evaluations – ideally before starting another piece of work – to see if the targets have been achieved and lessons learned.

Treat an evaluation as a continuing aid. If it does come at the culmination of the work make clear it is integral to the process, not simply something bolted on.

Link Sci-journal www.sci-journal.org/ then go to Hints and Tips > Evaluating
See also Appendix 10.

4
METHODICAL STRATEGIES

In this chapter we take a look at several information strategies in turn – and consider why it might be useful to develop your own. This would be a useful exercise to discuss in a staff working party. Remember that though each method may be laid out in a linear way, the process is actually a cycle, with 'finding out' leading to 'evaluation', then leading back to reconsidering the primary question or starting to tackle additional questions. It is less like a straight line and more like a circle with loops. The important thing is that all the stages be visited in an orderly way.

The Nine Question Step Plan is also given on the Strands table in Appendix 1.

Case studies

I asked several people who use information in the course of their work to describe their own methods. Some used methodical and efficient strategies while others believed they were successful intuitive information users who did not find it easy to detail how they went about an information-processing task.

Which of the following methods is most similar to your own practice?

Which do you think is the best model to follow?

Entry clearance officer

This person's job involves assisting British nationals in trouble and processing visa applications from people wanting to enter the UK. For this person's situation, information is mainly 'strict guidelines which enable you to make the correct decision within the law'.

Method
- Keep a log of information coming in (date, time and sign it).
- Ask for basic details (name, passport number, date of birth, contact details).
- Assess the urgency of the case.
- Make follow up calls and check databases.

- Get details of helpful agencies to pass on to informant.
- Call informant back with details of possible actions to take.
- Provide contact details in case they need further assistance and ask them to keep us informed of progress.
- Add all information including record of phone calls to database.

Managing director of training company

This person is responsible for company strategy and implementation in the light of global trends. For him information is 'the valid interpretation of data. Not a guess, and not speculative except as a means of uncovering possible alternatives that require further research'.

Method
- Identify the issue that requires the information.
- Identify what information is needed.
- Establish what sources we have in-house and where else to look.
- Seek help outside to isolate the people best qualified to give advice (resources).
- Seek their advice where possible.
- Narrow down the alternatives.
- Along the way, check attributable and unattributable sources including appropriate specialist libraries and the Web.
- Compare anonymous information with that gathered independently.
- Prepare a position paper for dissemination among interested parties.
- Decide on action or otherwise.

Consulting engineer

For this person information comprises material which is both published (e.g. internet, press reports, market surveys, patents, books, papers) and unpublished (e.g. information held by colleagues, third parties or on an internal database).

'Using information is absolutely fundamental to what I do. For example, I need to have background on what a potential new client company has been doing recently so that I can appropriately position a sales proposition to them. A second example would be a need to understand what's going on in a particular industry sector, e.g. who has been launching what new products in what markets.'

Method

'I first decide what I need to know, why I need it and who or what I'm going to consult. I tend not to define the task very rigorously as over-specifying it may lead to missing vital search areas. It's often better to talk simply in terms of why I'm looking for the information, and let the information professional help me formulate the search strategy and identify the best sources. Verifying the information is always important and absolutely essential in some cases. Everything must be fully verified and the sources recorded.

Once a client assignment has started, all information relating to the assignment is given a document number and stored electronically. Prior to that, I tend to store the information electronically in folders but in a less formal way.

Presenting the results of the information search is usually part of a much broader exercise – we are not simply finding information and passing it on to our clients, but using the information as part of a more complex deliverable, e.g. a new product design, a new manufacturing process or a report on the potential to exploit a particular technology in new market areas.

Evaluating the success of the task is initially by common sense, then by internal review and finally by seeking feedback from the client. All of our client work is subject to a quality control process in the form of a "Client Satisfaction Survey".'

Research scientist

'Research leads in unpredictable directions, and in order to interpret results and plan experiments, one has to know what others have found. If, for example, we discover that a particular gene or protein is involved in a process we are studying, we need to know what is known about that gene or protein – does it have a biochemical activity that would make sense? Like the blind men and the elephant, we tend to see only one part of a protein's function; to grasp the underlying principles one must integrate many apparently disparate findings.'

For this person there are two categories of information. One type is factual and closely tied to an experimental result, e.g. the amino-acid sequence of a protein, while other information is more abstract, and relies on interpretation, e.g. how the protein controls growth rate by degrading a protein required for cell division, or senses levels of nutrients.

Method
Sources Our major sources of information are the peer-reviewed academic literature and web-based databases that list experimental results and cross refer to the literature. Some of this information is partially incorrect, due to errors in the original data or in its collation. Experience tells us which databases are more reliable, and which journals have higher standards.

If investigating something far from my normal area, I find it best to consult a more knowledgeable colleague, who can provide that experience.

In more open-ended searches I may be unable to frame a specific question until I know what there is to ask. This involves repeated literature searches, looking first at titles of papers, then at the abstracts of the more relevant ones and only occasionally at the actual paper.

Verification How do I know what is correct? I rely on redundancy, looking for multiple independent papers that are mutually supportive and sometimes on my personal regard for the authors if I know them. The introductions to more recent papers will briefly outline what is known, and can indicate what past work is no longer taken seriously, but opinions differ and I always look at multiple papers to see what is common ground and what is presented differently by different people. Sometimes a fact is repeated frequently in reviews, but can be traced back to an old paper that, with hindsight, is not reliable, so key facts often need to be traced to their source.

Hypothesis. The goal is to construct a working hypothesis about my own studies, based on data from other systems. As this evolves, evidence that does not fit is examined critically and may be dismissed if, say, the interpretation is incorrect. This is necessary in order to produce a manageable and usable hypothesis.

Product For me, the output of these searches is not a concrete report (though I may use the knowledge in presentations) but a mental framework that is ingrained in my mind and used to plan further experiments. Success is a testable prediction that turns out to be correct. It comes from the integration of disparate data, often from studies of different types (genetic, biochemical) in different organisms. It allows progress to be made on a particular problem, and reveals both underlying common mechanisms and significant differences between systems. Integration of new results with existing information results in an improved under-standing, and provides the background information for the next round of discovery.

College development officer

This person's job involves writing publications, reports, raising funds for appeals, liaising with alumni, etc.

'Writing balanced articles about all sorts of topics I have to ensure that facts are correct before I disseminate them to others. Finding information about companies and people is useful for adding to database information. The database of alumni is a basic tool of the trade and is used to find people of certain skills, specific talents, career paths, etc.'

For this person, information is anything published in the public domain that increases or aids understanding of a certain topic.

Method

'The quickest medium is the internet and a search engine such as Google.

For example, I am looking to verify a student travel report for writing up as a fund-raising article. The student had helped at an orphanage in Romania. I am able to find a map of Romania. I am able to find the location of the orphanage and it may have a website. I am able to find information about Coucescou and why orphanages are a sad legacy of his regime. I am able to check the student's report and add some information so that the article is of more interest to a wider readership.

The facts in the article are thus verified, expanded and enhanced. It may lead to funds being generated as a result of a better balanced and informed report about student activities.'

Accepted models

It is clear from these examples that information users have different strategies and different understanding of the word 'information' and its use according to their work priorities. However, they use similar steps in their process. All of them frame questions, search a variety of sources, select and interrogate the resources they find, attempting to verify the reliability in a variety of ways then recording it before interpreting it for a particular purpose. Whether the source of information is an applicant, a knowledgeable fellow professional or a database, all the answers need to be filtered, assessed for their value and used with an end product in mind.

Whether we are working as scientists, diplomats, bureaucrats, engineers, authors, teachers or students; whether we are shopkeepers checking product trends, consumers choosing from a variety of products, readers of news comparing stories from different sources; we all need information strategies to cope with the deluge of often contradictory information.

How do you do it?

Below are some organized accepted strategies.

The Nine Question Steps

1. What do I need to do? (formulate and analyse need)
2. Where could I go? (identify and appraise likely sources)
3. How do I get to the information? (trace and locate individual resources)
4. Which resources shall I use? (examine, select, reject resources)
5. How shall I use the resources? (interrogate resources)
6. What should I make a record of? (record and sort information)
7. Have I got the information I need? (interpret, analyse, synthesize, evaluate)
8. How should I present it? (present, communicate)
9. What have I achieved? (evaluate)

Source: LISC Report 1984

These nine steps lay out the route very clearly, and give it both a simple question-based style and a more formal expression. However they are not memorable enough to be easily learned by pupils. They would be an excellent framework for lesson planning and learning resources, but nine is too many items to recall easily. Miller (1956) confirms that short-term memory can only hold between five and nine chunks of information and classroom experience suggests the lower end of the range is more likely.

The Eisenberg/Berkowitz Big Six Model of Information Problem Solving

1. Task definition

1.1 Define the task (the information problem)
1.2 Identify information needed in order to complete the task (to solve the information problem)

2. Information seeking strategies

2.1 Brainstorm all possible sources

2.2 Select the best sources

3. *Location and access*

3.1 Locate sources
3.2 Find information within the source

4. *Use of information*

4.1 Engage in the source (read, hear, view, touch)
4.2 Extract relevant information

5. *Synthesis*

5.1 Organize information from multiple sources
5.2 Present the information

6. *Evaluation*

6.1 Judge the process (efficiency)
6.2 Judge the product (effectiveness)

Source: Eisenberg and Berkowitz 1990

The six step plan appeals because six steps can be memorized (indeed a simpler three step version is apparently used in kindergartens in the USA).

However the six step route has become cluttered by subsidiary steps, making it more of a twelve step plan – which is too many steps to remember if used in full.

For more information on Big Six visit www.big6.com/

Five Steps to Research Success

Plan	(questions, strategies)
Find	(resources)
Work	(with the information)
Present	(the finished product)
Reflect	(how well did I do, what did I learn about both the subject and researching).

Source: adapted from Bloom's taxonomy in Susan Winebrenner's *Teaching Gifted Kids in the Regular Classroom.*

A GNVQ Model

Design an action plan
Identify information needs
Seek information
Select information
Synthesize
Communicate effectively
Evaluate

The above is a clear and straightforward seven step process widely used in vocational courses.

Three Big Steps

Preview
Do
Review

The above is a short basic list, suitable for younger children and for a quick fix.

What are the advantages and disadvantages of each model?

Take time to look at the models above and to decide what might work best in your school.

- The Three Big Steps might be best for younger classes or less able pupils. It is very simplified.
- The Big Six or The Nine Question Steps might be most suitable for more academic pupils on examination courses and adults. They may also form the framework of guided search worksheets with each step as a subheading followed by a blank box for pupils to enter their responses and their findings.

- All the strategies suggest there is a methodical approach to finding out, which is a good message to send irrespective of which method you choose.
- Arguments for and against each strategy can be distilled into 'Brevity versus Guidance'.
- The Big Six strategy has the most elaborate philosophy and strongest following in the US and Australia (mailing list, website) though it appears complex because it has too many subsidiary steps.
- Some strategies are written for teachers rather than pupils

Three new models

Having looked at the models above and considered their pros and cons I attempted to improve on them. The Hinchingbrooke Six Step Plan (below) is an attempt to bring the best of the models together and to use it in just one school. The present author gathered together a cross-curriculum working party, explained the background to methodical information literacy and offered the models above. The working party then came up with a model which they believed was understandable, memorable and could be used throughout an 11–18 comprehensive school.

We aimed to create something which was:

- memorable
- understandable
- listed the most important stages of the information process
- was no more than six items
- preferably created an acronym from its initial letters.

We compromised eventually by having something which has simple direct terminology and a built-in rhythm instead of an acronym.

This method has its faults – 'Do' (the task) and 'Answer' (the question) seem to be doing the same thing for tasks and for questions; 'reflect' is less precise and probably less often used than 'evaluate' – but if your colleagues will take ownership of one method, call it their own and be enthusiastic about its benefits, then it will be the best method for you. You can decide what terminology you prefer and how you want to present it.

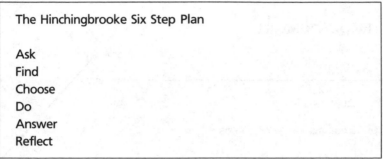

Source: created at Hinchingbrooke School, Huntingdon 1992

Having looked at the models above, here are two further models created by staff groups on recent courses.

The Need a Hand Model

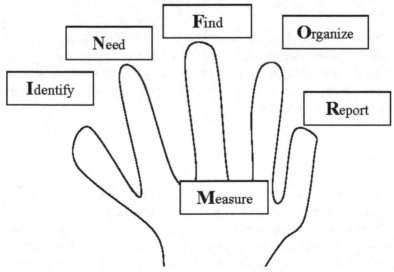

Source: created at Information Literacy Course, London, 2004

The initial letters on the fingers make the word INFORM so memorability comes from the clarity of language, the visual symbol of the hand (linked to the phrase 'Need a Hand') and the acronym INFORM. I think this is an excellent creation and well worth considering in schools.

The QUICK Model

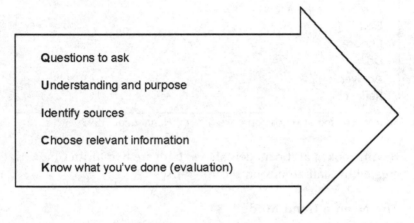

Questions to ask

Understanding and purpose

Identify sources

Choose relevant information

Know what you've done (evaluation)

Source: created at Information Literacy Course, London, 2005

The creators of the above model felt it could be designed around either a five-pointed star or an arrow. The acronym is successful and the visual impact could have good impact around the school, though the language does not have the strength and memorability of a single word.

Conclusion

I recommend both Quick and Need a Hand. However in the end I learned that the *product* is less important than the *process*. By discussing the idea together we created something which was our own and we were able to enthuse about it to other colleagues. So my conclusion is that *the best model is the plan you agree with your colleagues* and can implement successfully in your school. If your school has ownership of the model it will be more likely to improve pupils' learning.

Before you start creating your own version reread and discuss the models above and also the examples from the five professional information users, none of whom use these models exactly, but whose information strategies are based on practical experience and follow the same general pattern. The table below showing the steps, skills and processes of finding information might help too.

So, there's the challenge. Create your own and bring the rest of the staff on board instead of accepting an externally imposed model. Like a child, it may not be perfect, but the fact that you made it means you love it the most!

The Nine Question Steps	The information skills	The processing skills	The process
1. What do I need to do? (*formulate and analyse need*)	Questions Defining the task Making decisions Brainstorming		Compile key words Creating folders or directories named from key words or topics (see the main question)
2. Where could I go? (*identify and appraise likely sources*)	Problem solving Identifying sources		Saving 'favorites' websites to return to later
3. How do I get to the information? (*trace and locate individual resources*)	Locating sources		Copying, pasting or linking to relevant information within selected sources
4. Which resources shall I use? (*examine, select, reject individual resources*)	Selecting sources	Drafting and editing using cut and paste, drag and drop Note-making using highlighting	Including a citation of the source to avoid plagiarism and acknowledge the original work
5. How shall I use the resources?	Finding information within sources Reading for meaning Skimming and scanning	Creating annotations and	Reading the collected material and highlighting or extracting

The Nine Question Steps	*The information skills*	*The processing skills*	*The process*
(interrogate resources)	Evaluating material	inserting comments Creating hyperlinks	what is relevant and useful Checking and verifying the data
6. What should I make a record of? *(record and sort information)*	Note-making Sorting and arranging Developing ideas	Combining text sources (synthesis) Editing by search and replace	Highlight useful information
7. Have I got the information I need? *(interpret, analyse, synthesize, evaluate)*		Using tools such as the dictionary and thesaurus, the spell and grammar checkers, readability levels	Organizing the information under appropriate headings
8. How should I present it? *(present, communicate)*	Presenting findings Writing clearly Rhetoric Citing sources	Using typography, graphics and layout to enhance presentation	Writing, editing and synthesizing the data Presenting the finished product appropriately
9. What have I achieved? *(evaluate)*	Evaluation and review		Evaluating the process and revising if necessary Final evaluation

5

PRACTICAL STRATEGIES FOR IMPLEMENTATION IN YOUR SCHOOL

If you've read this far you probably have an interest in implementing an information skills policy. If you are one of the school's management team you might be in a position of influence but have too many responsibilities and not enough time. You could rely on a junior colleague to do the day-to-day work, or you might think of appointing a colleague to a position of responsibility such as Resources Centre Manager or Learning Coordinator.

If you are a librarian you might have information skills well organized in your school – or you might feel that you are not in a position to influence school policy. Nevertheless, many of the strategies below are focused on librarians who should play a key role in information skills.

If you are a teacher you might feel you can make a difference in your school by implementing some of these ideas, in your own lessons or in tutorial time.

If you are any of these, or an interested parent, governor, advisor or teaching assistant, you will find suggestions in this chapter for creating a cross-curricular information skills strategy. It will take several of you working together to implement it successfully, and you don't need to carry it all on your own shoulders.

SWOT analysis

An assessment of your Strengths, Weaknesses, Opportunities and Threats (SWOT) is a good way to start.

It is worth taking time to consider who is on your side, open to persuasion, keen to innovate? Talk to people generally and socially. Who would help, who might help develop an information skills strategy even if only by way of self-interest? Is the curriculum deputy an asset? What is the head's view? Who does he/she think could help you? Is there anyone who might make a noise on your behalf? Conversely, who might stand in your way, resist change, complain about curriculum developments, feel their power or position was being threatened? How can you appeal to the positive people and avoid irritating the negative people? Consider the Senior Management Team, heads of department, classroom teachers, support staff, governors, advertisers, inspectors, parents and pupils.

What opportunities are there to tie in to existing initiatives and objectives? Are there curriculum changes which might move things towards what you want, and can you get on board there? Are there building plans that might help extend your Resources Centre to provide a better collaborative environment, or funding changes which might provide improved resources or IT equipment?

Play to your strengths and try to minimize the negative. Stay positive. Always start with the people who are with you, and recognize that there are some who will never be convinced, but that the majority will come over to your way of thinking if your case is convincing enough and if it will benefit them, their teaching or their pupils.

Persuasion

This is the best way to get people on your side – though a little bribery with time, space and resources can also help. The ideal position is to be a Head of Resources at head of department level in the school and with capitation funding at your disposal. The following suggestions are based on this, but many of the suggestions will also apply to a librarian without a head of department role, a teacher without capitation or a deputy with curriculum responsibilities.

Persuasion means explaining and convincing colleagues of the advantages of information literacy. This would include the points listed below.

- Information literacy is a vital set of skills to enable pupils to learn and relearn in an information-rich world.
- Information literacy is a set of skills which all pupils need, which the National Curriculum enshrines and which individual departments have a responsibility to teach.
- The information literacy thread can be taught most effectively and economically by departments helping each other, build-

ing on the skills taught elsewhere and assisted by the librarians and the Learning Resources Centre.

- The Learning Resources Centre aims to provide resources in terms of facilities, personal assistance and materials for activities involving information literacy.
- The librarian is keen to help and give advice in planning lessons which involve information literacy and evaluating projects where appropriate.
- The librarian does not want to impose a methodical information literacy method but would like to work together with departments to agree on a united strategy.
- The librarian would welcome any interested member of staff to be part of a cross-curricular Library Resources working party, aiming to work together on a united information skills strategy.

Bribery

The points above would, I hope, be convincing on their own, but also include offers of time, space and money for resources.

Time

School librarians have time just when teachers do not. Teachers are more likely to be free at break and lunchtimes – just the times when librarians are at their busiest. Nevertheless, setting aside time to talk with teachers about their needs and hunting out relevant resources is time well spent and will be appreciated by any teacher.

A librarian's time during lessons, acting as an assistant teacher, answering pupils' resources questions, stressing the Six Point Plan, feeding back useful points about the skills the pupils have or do not have, is also time well spent. A librarian can see resources being used in action and can gather important information about the differences between what teachers say they need and what pupils say they want.

Space

This could be a quiet corner kept for a teacher to do preparatory work, or booking out most of the library for a whole-class project. A booking system will naturally favour those who have prepared their activities beforehand with the librarian and may alert those who are less well prepared to the need for organization.

Resources

Most librarians are delighted to be given suggestions for purchases. You might even send out a voucher for £50 or so to invite teachers to suggest books and resources for their departments. Naturally the final decision will stay with the librarian, and the stock should remain in the Learning Resources Centre, but there can be fewer things more guaranteed to appeal to interested teachers than the offer of free books.

If some teachers fail to respond even to this, then they are unlikely to be open to any of these suggestions.

And don't forget the power of tea and cakes to put people in the right mood for a working party meeting after school.

Working parties and committees

Being a member of an academic planning committee or an active curriculum working party provides all sorts of opportunities for the interested teacher or librarian to find out what's going on, suggest ways in which information literacy could be implemented and even to suggest how learning resources funding could be spent. Try to see where the curriculum thread connects up with suggested activities and say, 'While you're doing that perhaps we could connect up with . . .' or 'This would be an ideal opportunity to introduce some information literacy activities . . .'.

Very often a little preliminary research by pupils or a different kind of product at the end can satisfy your needs without any significant extra effort. As you become more experienced in the ways the curriculum works you could also suggest ways in which existing projects could tie in, to the benefit of all parties. Surely a local study could involve both history and geography. Could some environmental science be added? Could a diary of the project be presented for English, or ICT, or art?

Timetabling

It may seem obvious that any extra subject, topic or theme added to a school timetable must do so at the expense of existing topics, because the curriculum covers 100 per cent of the available time. In fact this is not necessarily so. While public figures airing their views will bang on about the need for better understanding of law and the constitution, road safety, exotic languages, en-trepreneurial skills and so on, all of which would take up extra time, the remarkable thing about information skills is that, as the extracts in Chapter 2 show, information skills are already in the curriculum, should already be taught and therefore do not need significant extra time.

What they do need is to be highlighted and taught in a methodical way across the school instead of being skated over in separate parts of the curriculum so that they are not seen as being part of an integrated curriculum. In this way they are typical of a significant weakness in pupils' experience of schooling – they simply don't see the connection (in secondary schools at least) between the different chunks of learning they are faced with lesson after lesson. And why should they when daily they experience regular chunks of teaching punctuated by a bell, a huge reshuffle and another wholly unrelated hour of something entirely different?

So timetabling is not really the problem here. What is necessary is for a mapping exercise to show where each of the information skills is taught and when. Using one of the methods I have suggested elsewhere and consistent terminology, pupils may see that a skill taught in one lesson connects to a skill taught in another and realize that the teachers are actually heading in the same direction.

Policies

Policies can be dull things, dusted off for inspections then hidden away again.

But they can be a stimulus for change and a reference for action.

I strongly suggest you formulate a library/resources policy as in the example given in Chapter 6. Discuss it with the library/resources working party and amend it as you see fit, then bring it to the attention of the head and if possible feature it in an academic planning meeting, management meetings or staff meetings as appropriate.

But that is not enough. It is a springboard for change, not a slab of stone. Push for your policy to be included in the overall school policies referring to teaching and learning. Then try to get every subject department to include a reference to library/resources and information literacy in their own policies. With these in place it should be possible to see whether teachers are adopting the basics of information literacy, making positive use of the Resources Centre and if they are not, to refer them to the various policy statements. There is no guarantee that all teachers will see things the same way as you, but with these policy statements in place you have made a mark and you can have some expectation of commitment.

Personality

Finally, yet crucially, the personality of the librarian is vital. If you have a vibrant personality, an excellent academic background and a strong position in the school – what are you waiting for? If you don't, you will need to enlist the help of others – which will make your initiative more successful in the long run. If you lack confidence in some areas this doesn't mean that you can't go ahead with implementing an information skills policy – far from it. It does, however, mean that you should conduct a SWOT analysis of your own strengths and weaknesses, play to your strengths and find someone else to supplement your weaknesses.

If your strength lies in a knowledge of books and search techniques but a weakness is your status in the school hierarchy, look around for someone to support you – a keen head of department, a curriculum deputy, the headteacher. You can help them by guiding them and advising them using the knowledge and skills you have, while they use their influence on your behalf.

How do you do this? You talk to your line manager and you play to your strengths, whatever they are. You provide the answers, materials and know-how while the 'front man/woman' pushes for you. Your resources working party, fuelled by your attention and your biscuits, can present your case in many areas of the school and will come back to you for support, advice and materials.

Find out what's happening next in your school's plan. See how you can offer advice and resources, time and bookings for a meeting, a new syllabus, a new member of staff, a new initiative. A solution to a problem, answers to questions, practical provision of resources for all occasions – these are the ways in which you can make yourself invaluable.

As I was advised by a wise older teacher, 'If you want to get on, make yourself invaluable; if you want to get out, make yourself superfluous.'

Action plan

While the Information Skills Strand is the most convincing piece of evidence to bring other teachers on board, there are also other ways:

Spread the word

- Compile an Information Literacy Policy.
- Get references to information literacy in every department policy.
- Create a representative Learning Resources working party.
- Create and implement a Five/Six Step Plan together.

- Offer a timetable slot in the Resources Centre for interested teachers.
- Offer to teach the first stages of information literacy (with teacher in attendance).
- Offer to support teachers with resources.
- Anticipate teachers' needs and surprise them with suitable resources.
- Provide displays of your resources linking in with curriculum work, then invite classes with teachers to see your displays.
- Offer study support after school.
- Monitor pupils' progress in using information skills.

Offer to help

- Find out who is sympathetic and work with them. Provide for them, help *them* boast about what *you've* done together and they will convey your success to the next person.
- Talk to teachers, find out what they want and need in terms of resources.
- Talk to pupils, find out what they want and need in terms of resources and (sensitively) about what is happening in their classrooms.
- Use five-minute slots in meetings to advertise your plan.
- Offer staff training.
- Help create curriculum projects with an information literacy framework, throughout the school.

Infiltrate

- Make a curriculum inventory of information literacy skills – for each year.
- Emphasize the National Curriculum strand regarding information literacy.
- Make sure the Resources Centre features on the website and intranet.
- Link from the school intranet and website to the Online Public Access Catalogue (OPAC).
- Link to suggested search engines and sites for information (see

122

Duncan's Essential Reference Page at www.putlearningfirst. com/dunk/ref.html).
- Find out about school, local and national initiatives which might provide a hook for your work.
- Offer to write relevant resource or information-based articles for the school magazine, parents' letters, website and local publicity.

An information audit

This chapter is mainly about information skills for pupils. Teachers of course can benefit from the same methods, and, if convinced, will not only gain personally but be more likely to enthuse their pupils. But what about your institution?

There are few schools, colleges, companies or local authorities that could not gain from an information audit. Ideally an audit will encompass all aspects of an organization, but here I want to dwell only on the practical movement of information in and out of your school.

Starting with your own personal information flow I assume that you receive information from phone, television, radio, websites and associated technology, email, paper-based mail and from other people.

You will respond to this by, for example, replying to some, storing the information from others (either in your own memory or in a filing cabinet) and ignoring the rest.

In many cases you will respond to a phone call by phoning back, to a text by texting, an email by replying and a letter by writing back. Sometimes you'll have to type out parts of a printed letter or a fax to reply by email. You may store electronic messages on your computer, print important things to go in the filing cabinet or scribble parts of text messages on a scrap of paper. Mostly that works pretty well because you are in control and can judge what goes where, how important it is to be kept and responded to promptly.

Scale up to a large school or a local authority, however, and a more coherent system is required. Many of the same media may be used – websites and associated technology, email, paper-based mail and information from people both official (advisors, inspectors) and unofficial (parents, teachers, pupils). Input may come to many different places – a head of year, a teacher, the school office, the head, the caretaker. Output and responses will be complicated, with the need for official documents, reports and answers that need input from several people and then must be synthesized and formally approved. The information process is complex and needs to be methodically organized.

Data collection

Schools collect and store data using the Common Basic Data Set (CBDS). CBDS is a set of data definitions or a data dictionary and not a list of data that should be held by schools. It provides a standard for data used in school, education authority, the DCSF and other software systems for management information. In this way data can be transferred between different systems in different institutions.

The CBDS uses unique pupil numbers (UPN), and records pupils' absence and attendance at school, exclusions data, pupil first-language data and other personal data about pupils, parents and staff.

Under the Data Protection Act 1998 all schools processing personal data must comply with the eight enforceable principles of good practice. Data must be:

- fairly and lawfully processed
- processed for limited purposes
- adequate, relevant and not excessive
- accurate
- not kept longer than necessary
- processed in accordance with the data subject's rights ·
- secure
- not transferred to other countries without adequate protection.

To comply with these principles every school processing personal data must notify under the Act. Failure to notify is a criminal offence.

How else might we take some control of this information flow while making the most of the information in and checking the quality of the information out without duplicating it unnecessarily?

Key questions

- What information do we need to meet our objectives?
- What information do we need to comply with legislation?
- What information are we creating, storing, processing and using?
- How effectively does information flow within the organization?
- How effectively does information flow between the organization and its external environment?
- What policies, actions and methods would improve the effectiveness of our information use?
- Are we using ICT effectively to manage our information?

Symptoms of poor information use

- Decisions are made based on information that is not the best available.
- Too much staff time is spent on information management activities (sourcing, storing, locating and retrieving) instead of core activities.
- Banks of underused information are dispersed around the organization.
- Critical information is not available when and where it is needed.
- Information creation and acquisition activities are often duplicated.
- Staff lack information handling skills – they don't know where information is held or what to do with it.
- The organization lacks common processes for managing information.

The information–poor school

A typical information-poor school will:

- have staff who don't appreciate the potential of the school management system (or are not allowed to use it) and will rely on support staff or senior management to extract it for them;
- believe it is overwhelmed with information when in fact it may be unable to discriminate between the useful and the superfluous;
- have ineffective policies to determine the information needed for government, local authority, staff, parents, pupils and how to get it there without unnecessary duplication;
- demand effective pupil reports from teachers but will fail to use technology to combine existing assessment data with personal comments to produce ready-collated individual reports;
- use a separate manual system for producing each bulletin and newsletter.

Possible developments

These would include:

- semi-automated information flows in report writing
- continuous online blogs for bulletins
- RSS feeds for news (RSS stands for Really Simply Syndication and is a way of publishing frequently updated content from sources such as news sites and blogs)
- CMS (content management systems) to discriminate between news for intranet, website and bulletins.

Other issues you need to deal with in school include privacy and security, identity theft, plagiarism and backups. These are management, personal information and ICT issues. Everyone in your institution must know about them and be active, for example, in preventing identity theft, encouraging good research practice and effective security of private information, while discouraging plagiarism and breaking of copyright.

The information-rich school

A typical information-rich school will:

- approach information in a holistic way, recognizing that the management and use of information affects the whole school;
- identify what information is needed and discriminate between what is needed and what is superfluous;
- use effective information systems that do not duplicate input but make efficient use of data to achieve goals and inform the education community;
- balance the need to know with the need for privacy and security;
- filter and direct information to appropriate audiences in appropriate ways;
- have policies on information privacy, security, access, use and plagiarism and actively put these into practice;
- have a staff who recognize the value of information skills and actively encourage these skills across the curriculum;
- make pupils aware of the value of information skills and put these skills into practice in their work and lives;
- recognize that the Library/Resources Centre can be an information hub for the school and value its service;
- comply with the Data Protection Act 1998.

Information privacy

With so much information about, much of it accessible all over the world on computer terminals and, increasingly, on mobile phones and similar portable devices, there is a significant risk of it being read by the wrong people. Or of being read wrongly by the right people. Of course people do consciously use the internet to publicize themselves, via their own websites or blogs or via social networking sites. As teachers we have a responsibility to warn our pupils about the dangers and consequences of this as well as of the obvious advantages.

Let's start with self-publicity. Using a camera phone a friend photographs you behaving badly under the effects of alcohol. What starts as an exuberant but fairly private evening out becomes potentially worldwide embarrassment when that photograph is uploaded to a website. If it's thought to be particularly funny or spectacular, especially if it involves nudity, it will not be long before millions of computer users have seen you, commented on you and forwarded the photograph or the clip to others. By the time you sober up everyone has seen you baring yourself to the world.

But embarrassment is only one consequence. When university admissions tutors and prospective employers compile short lists of job candidates they routinely search for online information. What will they think if the clip identifies you or if someone else's website links to you and your clip by name? What will they make of your 'crazy' entry in Facebook or MySpace?

Another consequence could be police action. If you are identified committing a crime you could be charged, using the photograph as evidence, and that is more likely to happen if you are identified as being under age. As the photograph can be stored locally as well as centrally and copied from one website to another, there is always a chance that this event can come back to haunt you later in life. Journalists looking for quick copy also trawl the web for information about you if you come to their attention.

Recently a man who deliberately broke his girlfriend's leg – with her agreement – as part of an insurance fraud, was given a prison sentence on the evidence of a recording he made of the incident using his mobile phone. A spokesman for Plymouth CID said, 'Only he knows why he decided to film it and provide the evidence which convicted him.'

The girl is no longer his girlfriend.

(Reported in *The Times* 21 November 2007)

Cyberbullying

One variant on information privacy is cyberbullying. It may seem fun to have innocent holiday snaps of you and your family on a social networking website but a recent phenomenon of cyber-bullying has been noted, with pupils searching the web for photographs of teachers or fellow pupils and then using them to embarrass or bully. It is a simple matter for photographs to be misrepresented alongside allegations of misconduct or of sexual innuendo. Embarrassing video clips can easily be circulated around the school and both pupils and teachers can suffer the consequences.

There are also websites that ask pupils to judge the quality of their teachers on a standard scale, adding unedited comments. Sometimes posing as a valued service to improve teaching standards these sites with their anonymous contributions can be professionally and personally embarrassing and offer no realistic right of reply.

Information security

The biggest information security failure in the UK was probably the loss of two CDs containing the confidential database of child benefit claimants from the HM Revenue and Customs Office in Washington, County Durham. Despite claims that security measures and procedures were in place, an employee down-loaded the whole database onto disc and sent it through the post to London. But it was lost in transit. The knock-on effect in terms of potential access by criminals to private information and bank accounts was massive. As the saying goes,'To err is human; it takes a computer to really mess things up'.

Where previously the loss of information from a locked filing cabinet would cause limited inconvenience, there is now the potential for unlocking vast quantities of information and using electronic tools to access online banking accounts or create false identities with global consequences. This comes about because previously disparate data is now connected electronically. The data is networked and therefore available from a wide variety of locations. A reliance on electronic identification instead of visual and personal inspection and paper documentation makes verification of data and identity easier to bypass.

We are victims of our own need for highly organized information systems.

Of course it should not be possible to download this data without authorization. The data should be made unreadable to someone without the necessary access permissions. However a combination of operator error and careless implementation of security procedures – inevitable human failings – allow it to happen.

The lessons this has for all of us are clear. We cannot put an absolute trust in electronic data. However, we can limit the risks.

Limiting risk

Encryption of data is a very secure method of keeping data safe. However this would arguably be too extreme for school and pupil data. In most cases a good password system and agreed behaviour, such as not taking crucial data away on a laptop or on a CD, would be enough. Aim to balance security restrictions with ease of access to those, such as staff, needing pupil information for report writing. Run a risk assessment.

Certainly use a secure password regime, limit its use to those who need to know and change it regularly. If you are responsible for a network, ensure the system requires users to change the password frequently. A secure password is one of more than six characters (longer is better) and uses a combination of upper and lower case letters and numbers. The difficulty of course is remembering it.

A good solution would be to choose a well-known phrase and use its initial letters to create a password. So 'Humpty Dumpty Sat On A Wall' becomes 'HDSOAW'. If we alternate upper and lower-case letters and replace the letter 'o' with a zero it becomes more secure: 'HdS0Aw'. Extend it to ten characters by using the second verse and we have 'HdS0AwHdHaGf'. Similarly the phrase 'Who Ate All The Pies' could become 'w8Atpiii'.

Both an unmemorable password and a recognizable password are failures. If you really must write it down, at least disguise it hidden within a phone or address list, not on a yellow sticky note in your diary or on your computer screen. By writing it down it immediately becomes unsafe. And if you have a large number of different passwords (because a single password would unlock a large number of your data sources) perhaps you should invest in a small metal safe (not forgetting the combination to that!).

An article, 'Top 10 most common passwords', claiming to be based on a sample of passwords appeared on the website Modern Life Is Rubbish (http://www.modernlifeisrubbish.co.uk/article/top-10-most-common-passwords). It claims the top ten UK passwords are, in descending order: 123, password, Liverpool, letmein, 123456, qwerty, Charlie, monkey, arsenal, Thomas. Other sources suggest 'admin' is the most common single password. According to this survey 1.8 per cent of people use one of the above passwords – and 6.5 per cent of people share a password from the top 100 list. The message is, if one of these is your password, change it quickly! A strong password will be long, random or known only by the user. If guessing it successfully will take the password cracker too long to work out, your data will remain secure. Try an online password checker to gauge the strength of your password.

Identity theft

Identity theft involves people collating some information about you and using that to create other pieces, usually with the final aim of stealing your money. This is not done by putting on a mask and muttering 'I'm Mr Grey, I want money from my account' but by using, say, a driver's licence and a birth certificate to open a credit card account in your name then spending money against that, which the credit card company will claim from you.

Identity fraud is a fairly simple thing to achieve. At one time the thief would raid your dustbin for discarded letters, utility bills, bank statements and receipts. Increasingly the data available online or via insecure sites makes rooting in bins unnecessary. Much of the information out there is provided by you and your friends. The rest comes from the bureaucracy of modern life – some of it, ironically, intended to make you feel safer.

The US Identity Theft Task Force report, *Combatting Identity Theft, A Strategic Plan* notes that during 2006, the personal records of nearly 73,000,000 people were lost or stolen (www.idtheft.-gov/reports/StrategicPlan.pdf). In the US in 2006 credit card fraud (25 per cent) was the most common form of reported identity theft followed by phone or utilities fraud (16 per cent), bank fraud (16 per cent) and employment fraud (14 per cent) (from www.consumer.gov 2006 report).

When asked for verification details on a shopping site you may be asked for your mother's maiden name or the name of your eldest child. This is inherently unsafe, because it can be found from other data. The first thing an identity thief will do is find out your family names and pet names and try these out. You yourself may even have publicized this information online, or a relative may have published your family tree.

Think also about the insecure information you carry about with you routinely. Look in your briefcase, handbag, wallet, purse, address book and notebook. Think about what would be lost if your Filofax or PDA (Personal Digital Assistant) was stolen. Not only would losing this be extremely inconvenient in itself, but the scraps of names, phone numbers, dates, receipts, cards, driver's licence, etc., would be treasure for a thief intent on identity fraud. In a short time you could find money missing from your accounts, with credit card bills, parking fines and summonses arriving for you – all because someone else has used your information to create your identity. And in this case much of the stolen information is not digital. The fact is that information is power, and power in the wrong hands can be used against you.

So don't unthinkingly give away information to the man at the door, the girl on the phone, the blank box on the tempting website or the spoof email pretending to be your bank. Check the veracity of the person and say you'll ring their company back. Examine the real URL of the link that seems to go to a national bank, and don't click it if it seems strange. Be sceptical about free offers and marvellous prizes that seem too good to be true. Never 'send to all your friends' some email warning but check it against known hoaxes at www.sophos.com/security/hoaxes/. And keep your wallet out of sight, your bag zipped up and on a strong strap, because information is valuable, whether digital or not.

In time we may be able to verify information by checking against biometric data. Voice recognition, fingerprint and iris scanning may tell the keepers of the data bank that you are who you say you are. This technology is already in use by UKVisas to identify applicants for visas and to avoid the situation where applicants apply several times under different identities to visit the UK. Fingerprint scanning is in use in some stores in Germany, and in some schools too, replacing debit cards and lunch vouchers as a means of payment. Whether biometric techniques ultimately make personal data more secure or, in their turn, provide a treasure house for criminals, only time will tell. Headlines such as 'Data loss anger' (*The Times* 23 November 2007) suggest that governments may have a hard job convincing people that data is secure.

Of one thing we can be sure. Information is valuable – to you, to the government, to the economy and to criminals. The more we know how to keep it safe and to make best use of it, the better.

Plagiarism

It has been said that when you 'borrow' from one source it is plagiarism, but when you borrow from many, it's research. There is some truth in this. Borrowing the ideas of others may be permissible but stealing the words they used to express this is plagiarism. Copying wholesale without adapting, interpreting or combining with other materials will be plagiarism.

It is a serious problem in relation to coursework and homework and is not unknown in classwork. Your school should have a policy which advises teachers on how to avoid plagiarism by pupils, how to identify plagiarism in pupils' work

133

and what to do if plagiarism is discovered. Examination boards all have procedures in place for suspected plagiarism and they are a good place to start when compiling a policy for your own school. There are many other policies available on the web.

The key points will include:

Pupils

- You must acknowledge the source of your material. Passing off someone else's work as your own is plagiarism – and plagiarism is theft.
- If you didn't write it, acknowledge who wrote it.
- Use quotation marks around in-line quotations of up to 40 words and indented paragraphs for longer passages.
- Avoid overusing quotations in your work and never use more than 200 words for a single quotation.
- Always include a bibliography in your research work.
- Be selective about copying and pasting from online sources.
- Remember that teachers and examiners want to know what you can do, not what someone else has thought or said.

Teachers

- Explain in detail to all pupils the school policy on plagiarism and the consequences of passing off someone else's work as your own. This could include reductions in marks, retakes, cancellation of exam entries.
- Set appropriate and individual tasks – which can't easily be copied. Avoid standard essays or add an original spin to the task.
- Make sure the question or task you set is answered and you don't accept a generic answer.
- Insist that originality is a prize – dull copying of the work of others is not educational. You would rather read their own thoughts than those of someone else.
- When marking pupils' work look out for unexpected stylistic and vocabulary changes that suggest someone else's voice.
- Suspicion of plagiarism must be followed up.
- Enter a suspect passage into Google or Google Scholar and

---

use quotation marls around it so it will be searched as a whole.
- Encourage your school to consider a licence for an anti-plagiarism website or software that tracks down the source of plagiarized writing.
- Consider your own use of online resources, photocopying, scanning and copying for educational purposes.
- Familiarize yourself with copyright regulations and ensure the school has a licence with the ALC (Author's Licensing and Collecting Society Ltd).

Garbled information

Accuracy of information is obviously important, and we must spend time comparing sources and cross-checking to evaluate what seems to be right. Checking the original source of information by using citations and references is the best academic way of doing this. But sometimes we ourselves introducing errors as we pass on the information we find and if we are teachers those errors are replicated in our pupils.

Which reminds me of Chinese whispers, in which, famously, the command 'Send reinforcements, we're going to advance', by frequent repetition became 'Send three and fourpence, we're going to a dance'.

If you'd like a quick and memorable exercise to use in class to demonstrate how information can become garbled as it is passed on, try the following. Think of a short phrase of, say, five words or ten syllables. Speak it quietly but clearly once only to a pupil and tell that pupil to pass it on similarly to another pupil. At the end of the chain compare what you originally said with what the last pupil heard. It's a good language lesson to trace back why one sound was misheard as another and a good example of information being corrupted as it passes orally from one person to the next. The same sort of thing happens as people interpret information differently and convey it imperfectly.

Backups

Another action you can take to keep your data secure, and prevent the pain of data loss, is to backup your work, frequently and regularly. Systems administrators may do this for us in a workplace, but it is our own responsibility to ensure that there is a copy of every one of our own files – a copy that is stored safely elsewhere.

A simple personal system would be to link your main machine to an external hard drive, which should have at least the same capacity as your main drive. Set a piece of backup software to copy either all your documents or, preferably, the complete contents of your computer to the external drive. Ideally you should have created a backup from which you can start up another computer if the main drive fails.

Backup software need not be complex and can be free or shareware. Mac users have a feature built in to their operating system which can even roll back the system to earlier stages to recreate a time before that vital file was deleted or before a power cut crashed the computer.

Backup software will allow you to set a quiet time, like early morning, when a backup can be made without interfering with your work. An incremental backup saves only those files that have changed since the latest previous backup, which is economical in time.

A removable hard drive allows you to take your data away to a safe place so there is a good copy in the event of total destruction of the original. A methodical backup system for a school's management system might include five removable drives, taken offsite daily and used in rotation to create a week's backups. This has been the saviour of databases that unknowingly became corrupted days previously but were not noticed.

At the very least, backup your current important personal files to a USB flash memory stick and make regular CD or DVD copies of other important files, including digital photographs.

Doing something as simple as sending a document to yourself as an attachment on web-based email preserves a copy online in case you lose the original. And don't forget your emails. Could you get in touch with that person if you lost their email address?

There are many other ways to keep backups, including uploading them to online web spaces. The bottom line is simple: any data backup is better than none.

Putting it all together

I've identified many features of a successful information-centred curriculum.

The main features are summed up in the figure below. 'A Six Step Plan' refers to the plan you chose in Chapter 2. It is the core around which eight other headings are grouped.

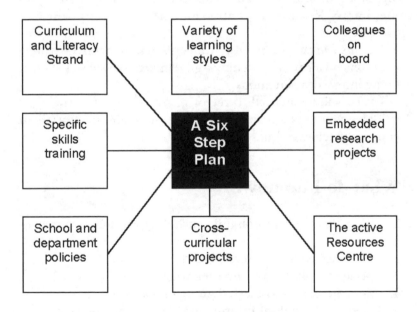

Information skills strategy

Your school's information skills strategy will incorporate all these features. It will do so by adopting a methodical information skills scheme, probably of six key steps. This will be official school policy, embedded in all departments' teaching schemes of work and taught by relating information skills to the normal subject content. Specific skills will be taught first discretely then integrated into subject areas in a variety of situations and using a variety of approaches and learning styles.

All teachers will be aware that other teachers are following the same scheme, therefore reinforcing their own work, and will appreciate how this follows the National Curriculum and Literacy Strategies.

Pupils will be explicitly aware of the coherent thread running through their lessons. They will see the six step plan on classroom walls and in their day books. Some classes will come across information skills in traditional classroom teaching, some in cross-curricular projects, some when they visit the library/Resources Centre for their frequent research activities.

Parents will be aware of the strategy and those who are willing may come to a parents' evening and reinforce the six step plan at home in practical situations.

Ofsted will be amazed. Director of studies ecstatic. The head will give you public praise. You will be typically modest about your great achievement.

What do I do now?

1. Read this book thoroughly, including the following chapters.
2. Pass selected ideas to colleagues.
3. Decide to talk to your line manager.
4. Get together an interested group of teachers.
5. Select a Methodical Information Plan or compile your own.
6. Spread the word!
7. Fill in your chosen activities in the flow chart below.

Read this material again?
Sketch out master plan?

Talk to line manager?
Talk to library staff?
Talk to teaching staff?
Talk to spouse?

Find interested colleagues?
Arrange first meeting to
discuss info steps?
Consider my preferred plan?

Produce an information pack?
Prepare a presentation?
Practise teaching some
info skills lessons?
Prepare posters?

And then?
Evaluate what you've done
so far and create some
new targets for yourself!

6

USING YOUR RESOURCES CENTRE AND YOUR LIBRARIAN

There are libraries, Media/Resources Centres (MRCs), Learning Resources Centres (LRCs) and Dead Book Stores. Libraries are good! Though because MRCs and LRCs have taken the glossy road to providing multimedia and interactive content, some good old libraries are suffering age discrimination, especially from a younger generation accustomed to fast results with resources that move and make noises. Dead Book Stores have, I hope, crumbled away. The change has taken place over some 20 years, with a recognition that there is a place for an information and learning centre, a hub where active, enthusiastic and self-directed learning can take place other than in a classroom.

In this chapter I am not ignoring the importance of fiction and reading for enjoyment. However the subject of this book is information and this mainly involves non-fiction. The best libraries will naturally try to encourage reading for pleasure and recreation as well as finding out.

The Resources Centre

Call it what you like, but this place can provide things your classroom cannot. There will be multimedia resources, book and non-book printed resources and in all likelihood a librarian who is both qualified and keen to help. If your school doesn't provide open access to a Resources Centre or has no librarian, start asking why. If the school is a small primary it can still provide a special area where pupils' attention can focus on reading and finding out. Perhaps parents and pupils together could help man it at lunchtimes. Otherwise it is hard to find a good reason for not having a thriving learning and information centre, where pupils can find out for themselves, be taught information skills to find out more effectively and learn because they are interested.

Your library should naturally be integrated into the curriculum and be a respected and accepted part of learning as well as reading for pleasure. A library policy (see below) should explain its role, aims, responsibilities and funding.

Perhaps you have some of these facilities within each classroom already. If so, you are extremely lucky, but the library still has an important role in addition to classroom provision. It is probably the only place where you have, all together, space for different kinds of work in small groups, an extensive and broad range of book and non-book resources, supervised by knowledgeable staff who are skilled in information skills and available throughout and beyond the school day.

The librarian

The librarian or Resources Centre manager is a teacher whose subject is learning itself. He or she is supported by library assistants, by well-selected pupil helpers and by all the staff in the school. The librarian is knowledgeable, friendly, helpful, sociable, hard-working and cooperative and knows that the best library is dedicated to learning. The librarian is there to help and to guide teachers and pupils to the resources they need. An excellent librarian can anticipate and satisfy teachers' resources needs.

If you don't recognize your library or Resources Centre in that description, you may want to refer to the following features.

Building blocks for library success

- Funding which is at least adequate, consistent and in proportion to department capitation.
- School management support and a line of communication which leads to and from the librarian to the top.
- A building that provides adequate space, storage and seating in a light modern environment.
- A strict weeding policy producing up-to-date and relevant stock which looks good and satisfies needs.
- A computerized catalogue which makes retrieval effective.
- CD-ROMs, DVDs, networked resources and internet sources, together with processing software which is fun, informative and practical.
- Book and non-book stock which meets curriculum needs and pupils' personal needs.

- Professional friendships with – and links to – departments and teachers.
- Resource-based projects which are well organized, the product of cooperation between teachers and librarians and embedded in the curriculum.
- A methodical ICT skills policy which affects every pupil and teacher – and curriculum time to enable it.
- A methodical information literacy policy which affects every pupil and teacher.

Learning in the library without walls

Learning in a library/Learning Resources Centre is different from learning in a traditional classroom, a traditional library or learning alone. An effective LRC has an effective librarian – 'a teacher whose subject is learning itself'.

An effective LRC believes:

- 'Give a child an answer and you tell him once; teach him how to find out and he learns for life.'
- 'Information is of two kinds: we know a subject ourselves or we know where to find information on it.'
- 'Education is about learning to ask better questions.'
- An LRC is by definition a centre but its influence does not stop at the loans desk – it extends to the furthermost extent of the school and the home.

Roles and responsibilities

A well-organized and well-resourced school should have a librarian or head of resources and several librarian assistants. They will aim to move beyond *passively* providing books towards *actively* creating learning opportunities, stimulating pupils to find out more for themselves.

Learning is a team effort, a learning partnership, with teachers and technicians, librarians and their assistants, enabling pupils to reach their learning potential. They may also use contacts outside school – help from the community, local authority advisors, sharing with other schools including feeder schools and other schools in the UK and elsewhere.

Teachers need and deserve help and librarians can provide it. This is the first step towards the partnership which leads to information literacy in pupils. Librarians are usually extremely keen to have their resources used and they have a thorough background of information use. Since librarians like to offer and give and teachers appreciate people who provide, here is the basis for a useful partnership.

Librarians can help

They can help by:

- Alerting teachers to new relevant resources. Perhaps a regular email resources bulletin. Anything to bring existing resources to the attention of teachers.
- Being ready to offer suggestions and show resources. Displays in staff rooms, casual meetings with interested staff.
- Offering to take the class for a short while – and the teacher will learn too.
- Offering to take part in school INSET.
- Keeping in touch with curriculum developments – membership of committees, being on circulation lists, having regular meetings with curriculum deputy and keeping in touch with DCSF initiatives via the TES.
- Offering holiday reading for teachers.
- Generating displays of resources and asking teachers for suggestions and advice, pandering unashamedly to those who are enthusiastic about information literacy and buying stock for the projects they intend to implement.

Teachers can help

They can help by:

- Building a good professional relationship with librarians and the Resources Centre.
- Using the LRC actively and positively, for preparation and for lessons.
- Making pupil use of the LRC a positive experience.
- Referring pupils, if appropriate, to the LRC during lesson time and trusting them to use it sensibly, making sure they are familiar with relevant stock.
- Using appropriate lesson and tutorial times to develop information skills.
- Providing the librarian with suggestions for new resources that will contribute to learning.

Why create more resources?

Why, when there are so many resources available commercially, do you need to create more?

- Because good teaching is *flexible* and *personal*.
- It uses the teachers' *enthusiasm*, *knowledge* and *interests*.
- It uses *local features*, *places*, and *characteristics*.
- It uses pupils' *previous learning* and develops their *skills* using their *interests*.

Commercial providers can only generalize about this. They take soundings from teachers and ask for advice but almost inevitably few teachers will use a published resource exactly as printed. It is more likely that a teacher will mediate the material, adapting it to immediate conditions and personal preferences. Even two teachers who have collaborated on producing a unit of work will end up using the material in different ways – indeed teaching is at its best when an enthusiastic teacher responds actively to a unique audience.

The kinds of unique resource that can be produced would include a well-organized clippings file using cuttings from newspapers to build up items of local interest. This can be a routine part of the librarian assistant's day, turning yesterday's news into tomorrow's resource.

Librarians and teachers can collaborate to provide relevant resources, which may enable a variety of learning objectives in lesson time, in tutorials and informally around the school. And pupils can collaborate with their peers in or outside the school to gather and share more information.

A local studies project is a good topic to collaborate on at many levels. Local schools can build up a collection of details which are relevant to themselves and nearby schools – and which may not be easily found outside the immediate area.

A project could involve the primary school as a critical audience for the secondary school's work. Design and technology classes can research designs and build a model of a playground. English classes can research stories appropriate to age groups, study writing styles and write stories for primary children, then hear their response and evaluate their work.

Use the Learning Resources Centre

The library/Learning Resources Centre is the obvious place for any research. In some cases, there may be more facilities in a computer suite, but it is important that the methods of information literacy apply. Some of the work can continue in the classroom, and some of the skills may be best taught first in class or in tutorials, but access to the Resources Centre should be available as much as possible.

Teachers can improve their use of the Learning Resources Centre by:

- creating an interesting and relevant set of introductory lessons to show pupils around the Resources Centre and how to use all the facilities. For example, give pupils a giant quiz to practise their finding-out skills. Or have one class compile a quiz for another (though check it carefully first!), which then gives feedback.

- Agreeing a methodical core curriculum to teach the basics of information skills.
- Adapting and improving existing projects to use information literacy methods to develop the core information skills.
- Creating new cross-curricular projects using information literacy skills.
- Buying stock appropriate to these projects.
- Creating a library/Resources Centre working party to develop a school information skills policy, to be adopted throughout the school with a Six Step Plan as a methodical information strategy.
- Identifying a leader and mover as a head of resources.
- Creating web pages on the school website linked to a range of essential resources. These can be used as a focus for resource-based learning and as part of the Resources Centre's contribution to the school website.

More information

The Booktrust www.booktrust.org.uk/
Book lists from Booktrusted www.booktrusted.com/
School spending on books
www.booktrust.org.uk/schoolspending/report.htm
The Book Check Assessor www.books-raise-standards.co.uk/
School Library Association www.sla.org.uk

A library/resources policy, created by teachers and librarians and formalizing strategies for working together, should be approved by the school management team, introduced to staff meetings and available to remind staff on how the Resources Centre and its staff can help staff and pupils alike. It should also formalize the school information strategies and the curriculum as it relates to information skills.

A sample library/resources policy

*What a school thinks of its library
is a reflection of what it thinks of education.*
(Harold Howe)

The library/Resources Centre is available for use by the whole school community, subject to standard rules and regulations given elsewhere. Where demand is too great a booking system operates for classes and a rota system operates for year groups at busy times.
  We aim to:

- meet the needs of the school community for information and literacy;
- provide computer software relevant to information retrieval and appropriate to the school's needs;
- ensure the Resources Centre satisfies the needs of pupils, staff and the curriculum, by:
    - monitoring use, stock and curriculum requirements
    - providing a balance of book and non-book resources and software appropriate to the school's needs;
- offer a service of advice, resources and expertise which will facilitate the development of flexible and resource-based learning;
- provide an atmosphere in which private study, quiet relaxation and personal enquiry can flourish together;
- provide the means by which every pupil and member of staff can become familiar with the methods of information retrieval.

This will include a continuing training programme for library staff by IT experts, for teaching staff by librarians, for pupils by staff during resource-based learning projects.

The teaching of information skills and familiarity with the Resources Centre, its stock and its organization are essential aspects of our role as teachers. The school has adopted an information skills policy.

These aims are met by:

- introducing each new member of staff to the Resources Centre as part of the induction procedures;
- holding weekly lessons for every Year 7 pupil starting with a basic introduction to the library and followed by a framework of information skills tasks and reading tasks;
- a Year 9 research project which is a six-lesson unit practising information skills within English lessons;
- other projects specifically written for departmental and pastoral needs and incorporating information skills tasks. The list of these projects is changing continually.

We ask that:

- heads of all departments communicate their needs to the librarian/head of resources;
- policy documents of each department will include a statement relating to:
  - the use of the Resources Centre
  - independent learning
  - information skills;
- teachers ensure the purpose and outcomes of pupils' research is clearly expressed and methodically carried out;
- notice of research be given to the librarian in advance wherever possible and properly designed research projects are planned together with head of resources or the librarians.

The head of resources is happy to work with subject specialists to produce such coherent projects and the necessary resources.

Funding

This is determined at the beginning of every financial year and is allocated on the basis of a 10 per cent share of school capitation.

> The intention of this is that the Resources Department should be treated equally fairly with other school departments, rising or falling with generous or strict funding allocations.

We encourage suggestions for additions to our stock from all pupils and members of staff.

The Resources Centre is a central facility for use by all pupils and staff. The librarians particularly welcome appropriate purchases suggested by departments and individuals who demonstrate active and positive use of the Resources Centre and its philosophy of independent learning.

The Staff Library

This is a facility for all staff to enhance their professional development. The materials in the Staff Library are funded from the Staff Professional Development Fund.

Responsibilities

- Responsibility for the Resources Centre is lead by the head of resources, who has a librarian and assistant librarians sharing the responsibility for the day-to-day running of the centre.
- The head of resources is responsible for the curriculum and thence to the headteacher.
- The head of resources is in close contact with the head of ICT who advises on computer needs, their use and their purchase.

Maintenance

Maintenance of different parts of the school and equipment is the responsibility of various members of staff:

- the stock room is maintained by the librarians;
- the PCs and the network hardware are maintained by school IT technicians;
- the library catalogue software is maintained by the software helpline.

Relationships with other organizations

- The librarian attends meetings of other librarians organized by Schools Library Service and meetings of the library software users group.
- The Resources Centre is committed to supporting the County

Schools Library Service and pays a subscription which provides access to support and advice as well as to resources for pupils.
- The Resources Centre is a member of the Schools Library Association and pays subscriptions to them and to the Library Association.
- The Head of Resources is a member of the LM_NET and SLN librarian networks.

Job specifications

These are given in a separate document, modified in the light of the Librarians' Annual Review in July (q.v.).

Plans and reviews

Development plans for the year are given to the senior management team annually. In addition a Librarian's Annual Review is produced at the end of the academic year, following department discussion and evaluation.

This policy can become a powerful tool for positioning the library/Resources Centre in the heart of the school and integrating information skills into the curriculum. It will need annual revisiting to ensure that teachers and their departments are pulling together in the same direction, but I am convinced that once teachers see the benefits of sharing resources, agreeing a common strategy and making active use of the librarian and his/her stock, there will be no serious barrier to development.

7
SEARCH ENGINES AND COMPUTER SKILLS

Searching for anything – whether a spare sock or the answer to the meaning of life – involves formulating a question before you start. Otherwise you'll never know if what you find is what you want. Formulating a search means asking the right questions. This can be taught in any and every lesson. In practice choosing some appropriate key words will help in any catalogue or search engine. Checking that these words are appropriate and that their spelling is correct will make your search even more effective.

Search engines

Data is either indexed by robots who trawl through the text and use algorithms to sort and rank the results, or arranged in a catalogue by human editors. A search engine differs from an index in that it can be searched using key words and is not a fixed list, as is the index to this book, for instance. The engine creates a complex searchable database.

Google www.google.com/

Google is the most popular and probably the most powerful indexing search engine. It sends electronic 'bots' to visit the world's websites; stores, ranks and indexes them but does not evaluate them. You can search Google using key words and using advanced search you can include and exclude particular words and phrases.

Other general search engines include HotBot, Lycos, AltaVista, Ask and Excite. There are countless other specialist search engines. Visit www.searchengines.com/ for examples. Some of these engines search through the complete text of web pages (whole text search) while others store key words. Whole text can throw up irrelevant results but is more complete, while key word search depends on the quality of input by the author of the key words.

iTools www.itools.com/

iTools offers different search boxes so you can decide whether to search the Web, Google video search, ask other people, web directory, discussion groups or to find people by name. This guidance can help by narrowing down your search and by searching sources which are not commonly listed. It also offers links to specialized searches for languages, research, finance, maps, etc.

Noodle Tools www.noodletools.com/ (click on 'Choose the best search')

Noodle Tools defines and tries to clarify your questions even more. It uses headings such as 'I need help to define my topic' or 'I need quality results' with subsections such as 'I need a topic', 'I need to understand the scope of my topic' or 'I need to investigate alternative or related topics'. It then guides you to a specialized search engine and describes its advantages. If nothing else, by posing questions to you it forces you to clarify your thoughts. A visit to Noodle Tools would be a useful school trip.

Yahoo www.yahoo.com/

Yahoo is a web directory. Editors select the information in these directories and arrange it in a hierarchy from a general top category, down through detailed subcategories. You can search Yahoo by using key words or by drilling down through the categories getting more and more specific.

Subject gateways or portals

Subject gateways or portals are like directories in that they are collections of websites arranged under subject headings. They specialize in a topic or a particular field of knowledge. They are often selected by experts and you can check the editors or publishers to see if they are credible sources. As they are often selected by individuals it is important to check that they are up to date too.

Search words

Search words, otherwise known as key words, tell the search engine what you're looking for. Most search engines will ignore words such as 'on', 'the' and 'of'.

If it is important that a phrase is found exactly as written, place it in 'quotation marks'.

To be more precise in a search, choose Google Advanced Search and select whether your search should include *all* of the words, with the *exact phrase,* with *at least one* of the words or *without* the words.

Choosing an appropriate key word is a vital skill if you are to achieve a successful search. Sometimes we need to know more about a subject before we are in a position to choose the best key word, so several searches at different stages in the process can be helpful. Pupils should consider which words are most important and accurate in describing the topic. They should also try synonyms and both singular and plural forms of words. For example, the key words 'mathematics', 'maths' and 'numeracy' will produce different search results.

This is a good activity combining English (choosing appropriate vocabulary), mathematics (compiling charts of success rates for searches using different search terms) and information skills (assessing the success of finding appropriate answers to your questions). The activity could cover several search engines and several other media (CD-ROM, encyclopedia, non-fiction index).

Improving your searches in Google

Google's mission is 'to organize the world's information and make it universally accessible and useful'. Many of the tricks below also work in other search engines. It is always useful to compare different engines and their success rates. Remember that 'less is more'. Finding a million examples in your search is not a success, it's a failure. Finding a small handful of highly appropriate results is just what you need. The way to do this is to refine your searches so they give you exactly what you were looking for.

Quotes

Place 'quote marks' round the exact phrase you're searching for. 'Quote marks' will find only those words together, while searching for *'quote'* and *'marks'* will find those two words separately. You can also use this technique to search for a part-remembered phrase.

For example, I may know the quotation begins with 'education is what is left when' and I think it ends with 'has been forgotten' but I'm not sure of the exact words in between. Searching for the first phrase brings up 1,890 items; searching for the second phrase brings up 303,000, while searching for both – each in their separate quotation marks – brings up just 24.

This shows me that the missing words from the quotation could be: 'what has been learnt', 'what was learned', 'everything else', 'everything that has been taught', 'all you have learnt', 'the subject matter'. I eventually decide I prefer 'Education is what is left when what is learnt has been forgotten' (B. F. Skinner). Of course by searching for any one of these using quotation marks I would have missed all the others.

Plus and minus

If there's something you definitely want to appear in your search add a + sign in front.

So +*bucket plastic* will show only pages where bucket appears and won't offer you general stuff made of plastic.

Similarly *bucket -plastic* will give you examples of buckets but not plastic ones.

Duplicating

Crude but simple: enter the most important word twice in the search box. *Bucket bucket* adds importance to the word. But don't overuse it – two instances of the word is enough!

Synonyms

Put a tilde (~) in front of words when you want to search for a word of the same meaning. So *~maths* will find 'arithmetic' and 'numeracy' too.

Or

Place 'or' between two words and Google will find either the first or the second. This could be useful for US/UK spellings (*colour or color*) or US/UK vocabulary (*car or auto*).

Define

Type 'define:' followed by your text and Google will search for definitions. Don't forget the colon. *Define:internet* gave 27 definitions and their sources plus related words.

Calculator

The Google Calculator can perform simple and complex mathematics including converting units of measurement. Enter *12% of 89* in the search box. Not only will it give you the answer but it will provide a link to more details of the calculator functions as well as documents containing the phrase. Or enter *half a cup in teaspoons* (the answer's 24). Brilliant!

Search within results

Sometimes you find so many results that you would like to refine them. Instead of starting the search all over again go to the bottom of the first Google page where you will find a much ignored search box already populated with the words you've been searching for. Next to it is a link saying 'Search within results'. Instead of entering new search terms you can simply refine the large number of answers you've already found.

Advanced and further features

Google also offers *Advanced Search* for more complex and detailed searches.

Google offers Image Search to look for pictures and graphics. Note that the advanced choice in Image Search has a filter of three levels: 'no filtering', 'moderate' or 'strict'. Schools should have this set to 'strict' and if possible keep this page banned from pupil use, otherwise a pupil could reset the filter to 'no filtering' which allows pornographic pictures.

Google has a host of other services and information tools such as Map and Earth showing maps and aerial views and Google Scholar which is excellent for citations and references.

Library catalogues

Electronic catalogues normally work in a similar way to internet search engines, in that the user enters appropriate key words and the search facility matches the user's key words to those held in the catalogue. They may also use Dewey numbers and even show the shelf position of the resource.

Library catalogues usually concentrate on books but many can also index non-book resources including selected websites. A school librarian can therefore complement the book stock by choosing appropriate additional websites.

Traditional paper or card index catalogues also require some idea of key words if they are to be useful, so key words are an essential first step in searching.

Processing

Having found your raw material, the next step is to process it. Processing your data can be done using one of the methodical strategies detailed earlier, but dealing with the content can be made much easier using electronic tools. Word processing electronic data, using a database or spreadsheets and graphical organizers can in turn lead to a presentation.

Other ICT tools

Collecting, storing, organizing, editing and presenting information can be done with traditional pen and paper tools – but computer software has made these tasks considerably easier.

Traditional tools include files, folders and wallets to gather together the cuttings, jottings, notes and drafts, separated perhaps by dividers. Pencils and coloured pens allow you to distinguish between different topics, comments, explanatory notes, etc.; highlighters emphasize and select; a single line through text shows it is unwanted while still remaining visible if you change your mind. Shuffling separate pieces of paper can reorder information into topics and making notes on separate cards allows for a more organized retrieval system. Cutting up paragraphs and reordering them can also help achieve the right sequence. Photocopies, carbon paper, paper and bulldog clips, sticky labels and coloured tacky notes all help at the time when everything needs to be laid out on a long table and put into the right order.

Software often replicates these tasks, improves upon them and sometimes creates new and more efficient ways of working. The following examples are mainly free or shareware and are constantly being supplemented by new ideas and new ways of working. Visit a shareware archive such as Tucows (www.tucows.com) or Download.com (www.download.com/) and look for 'desktop enhancements' or 'productivity enhancements' for any number of clipboard, note-making or text-moulding programs. What seems puzzling and unnecessary to one person may be the quirky solution to all the problems of another person.

Desktop features

These will depend on your operating system but could include multiple desktops (use a different screen for a different project), customizable filing systems (using icons, labels or colours to identify folders and files), ways of conveniently laying out frequently used programs and files and so on.

System preferences and control panel settings mean you can create a convenient and comfortable environment while you work, while spam filters and virus checkers keep the machines safe.

The Google toolbar and the Mac Dashboard add an extra layer of widgets to your desktop with small but useful software enhancements.

You can also 'lock down' a desktop, or create a restricted account, so that young fingers don't upset the balanced environment you have so carefully created.

Web browsers and extensions

As so much research takes place on the Web a browser is essential. But you need not use the browser that comes with your machine by default. Microsoft Explorer faces fierce competition from Mozilla Firefox amongst others, which has a wide range of plug-in extensions so you can choose to create a well-functioning window on the Web.

Setting your browser preferences can make a big difference to your browsing experience. You may prefer a clutter of different windows or a series of tabs within a frame, you may prefer one video or audio player over another, or have preferences for certain text sizes.

Organizing 'favorites' or 'bookmarks' and deleting various toolbars will certainly save time and make life easier, and the size of the cache (memory store) you set may mean you can go back in the history of pages visited and find a vital site. Security and privacy settings will need checking too.

One plug-in I use to organize web pages and documents is

Zotero, a Firefox extension to help you collect, manage and cite your research sources. It sits in the web browser itself and offers automatic capture of citation information from web pages. Google Notebook does something similar and enables sharing of your notebooks with others.

RSS

An RSS feed automatically delivers news to you from single or multiple sources. You will need an RSS reader, which can be a stand-alone program but increasingly can be conveniently set in your own home page (iGoogle is a good example) or are embedded elsewhere in your browser. Choosing an appropriate RSS feed means you can be kept up to date with new developments without having to go out and search for them.

Email tools

Whether you use web mail or a dedicated email program such as the ubiquitous Outlook or Outlook Express, the way you arrange your subfolders into helpful topics, how often the software polls the server to check for new mail, whether you keep your mail on a distant server or download it to your computer – will all affect your efficiency and enjoyment of receiving and making the most of mail. You may have to fine tune the settings to filter out spam, may have to spend time organizing and checking your address book and contact groups and will have to decide how to store mails and attachments if they are to be accessible later.

Don't forget also to use email headings or titles which make sense so you can recognize and retrieve them later. Keep the same title when replying to a message so there is a link between a series of messages. Archive old mail so it doesn't clutter up your inbox.

Personal home/start pages

Your choice of home page will affect your work. In a school this may be the school home page, but does it give ready access to a page of information tools? Can staff easily get to the private virtual staffroom? Can all users easily reach the intranet, school calendar, library catalogue?

VLEs (virtual learning environments) usually provide personal home pages for each user, but how easy are these to customize and what advice is given as to the essential elements that must remain?

iGoogle and Pageflakes are examples of highly flexible personal pages that offer access to movable panes containing RSS feeds, calendars, news, favourite links and 'gadgets' such as search tools, weather forecasts, calculators, random web cams, etc.

Organizing a home page can improve your work flow – or prove a never-ending distraction.

Search and research tools

I would always provide a range of search engines on a school website or personal home page because they have different strengths. I like Noodle Tools www.noodletools.com/ as well as Google; I use Google's specialized searches (image, scholar, books, etc.) as well as the standard page search; a thesaurus, Wikipedia and a dictionary are also important to my searching.

Text processors

Word processors have changed the way we write and the way we organize text. Hypertext links have changed the way we relate text, graphics and ideas and arguably have changed the way we think. Even the simplest text editor can be used to reorder ideas by cutting and pasting sections of text. Since there is no need to rewrite after every edit and a series of easily made copies preserves drafts, writing is made a good deal easier. Separate notes written swiftly in a basic text processor can later be simply reordered and combined in a word processor to create a longer piece or stored in any number of organizers to create an information bank. Scrivener (www.literatureandlatte.com/scrivener.html) does this within a single program. Hyperword https://addons.mozilla.org/en-US/firefox/addon/1941 is a Firefox plug-in that adds inter-activity to any word by providing a drop-down menu to look up, search, reference, translate, paste or email any text in a browser window. As a complement to your chosen word processor it adds exceptional functionality – and it's free!

Fully fledged word processors, of which Microsoft Word is perhaps the most famous, but Open Office (www.openoffice.org/) is a good free equivalent, and related software such as web-page editors and page-layout programs have a long list of tricks available to make information more expressive, readable, presentable and easier to repurpose.

Consider drag-and-drop editing, find and replace, highlight-ing, autosummarize, track changes, document merge, scrapbook, built-in reference tools (dictionary, thesaurus, encyclopedia), customizable toolbars and key strokes, styles, indexing, table of contents, hyperlinks, graphics, comments, tables, etc.

Organizers

- A good word processor can be a useful organizer in that while its main strength will be text, most processors provide for insertion of objects such as graphics, tables and formatting tools plus search and replace facilities.
- Presentation software and photo organizers also have features to arrange graphics in a variety of ways. Apple's iPhoto and Adobe's Photoshop Express (http://www.photoshop.com/express), for example, offer cataloguing and indexing, sorting photographs by topic or theme, editing tools to enhance, crop or filter the photographs themselves and slideshow tools with fades and music for quick presentations.
- Dedicated presentation software, of which PowerPoint is best

known, integrates multimedia using a slide-based metaphor to produce slick and adaptable presentations.

- Spreadsheets and databases are very powerful organizers, making it simple to enter key words or other data and reorganize it in predetermined fields for different purposes. Where the early dictionary compilers struggled with separate sheets and cards of definitions in thousands of wooden pigeonholes a spreadsheet or a database can resequence each record while keeping each field editable.
- Content management systems, some of which are based on blogging tools, allow even greater flexibility in arranging and publishing large numbers of news items, documents and resources. Mind-mapping software, by connecting separate documents or ideas in a visually understandable way, can be inspirational and genuinely creative.

This is just a brief glimpse of currently available tools designed to help arrange and make sense of the information we need. By the time you read this there will, no doubt, be even more tools available, because software designers know that collecting, storing, organizing, editing and presenting information is a task for which we all need help.

Presentations

Presentations vary according to need and the media used. A printed essay with tables may also be presented as a series of slides with graphs and a spoken commentary, and repurposing information in different forms for different audiences avoids a total rewrite.

Presentations can be made in a variety of forms.

In medium:

- printed
- electronic
- oral.

Delivered:

- on CD, DVD or other electronic storage medium
- web pages (online or offline)
- hyperlinked files
- projected slide shows
- podcasts.

In appearance:

- text
- graphical
- tabular or columnar
- animated
- hyperlinked
- with sound
- multimedia
- interactive.

Created using:

- pen and paper
- word processors
- graphical software
- paint or photo software
- spreadsheets
- databases
- dedicated presentation software
- film editors
- podcast and audio editors.

Moreover, almost any of these can be used in combination, so the choice is extensive. Marshall McLuhan famously said, 'The medium is the message', however, the priority must remain the content of that message, with the medium enhancing the message not detracting from it or being there for its own sake. If, following a presentation, the audience only remembers the flashy graphics and weird effects, the presentation has been a failure. If the message is enhanced by explanatory animations or made more convincing by graphs and charts, then that presentation is a success.

The future

I can confidently predict that search engines will become faster and more effective at finding things for us, learning from our previous searches and suggesting what they think we want as well as what we say we want. They will also probably try to present that information in more accessible ways using graphical methods like the VisuWords graphical dictionary (www.visuwords.com) to create a semantic web with visual relationships between topics.

Overleaf there is a graphic representation by Visuwords of the word 'information' with some 40 varieties of meaning. Differently shaded circles show nouns, verbs, adjectives and adverbs while differently coloured lines indicate 'is a kind of', 'is a part of', 'is similar to', 'also see', 'derivation', etc. Informative as this certainly is, it is as nothing compared to the way the words and pop-up definitions appear on screen floating and undulating around the browser window.

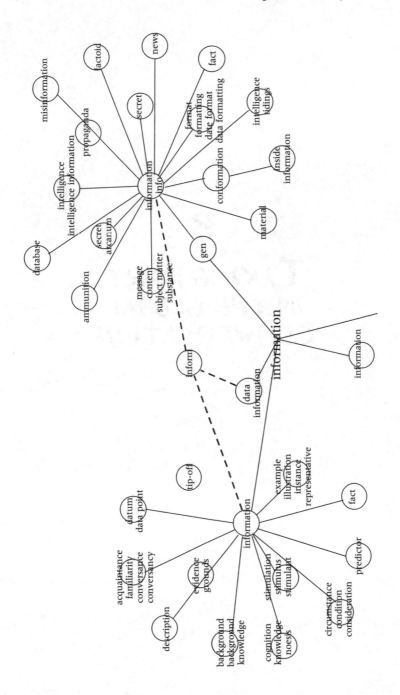

8
TAKING PART IN THE GLOBAL CONVERSATION

Just as desktop publishing enabled individuals to publish their own writing without intervention from commercial publishers, the internet is a vehicle for publishing to a global audience. Since the mid-1990s it has become increasingly easy to have your writing appear on web pages around the world. Whether it has become easier for people to find it and whether people will read it once they have found it is another matter. Just as the more you shout the less folks listen, it seems the more you publish the more your readership becomes blind, or at least immune to your work.

So while the traditional book trade continues, helped in some ways by a global book shop and by electronic publishing tools, the voice of the non-professional author can be heard too. Information has become not only something which happens 'at' you, but something you can contribute to. It is this modal shift which is at the heart of the information revolution. We can not only read comment and opinion by journalists and pundits but we can express our own views too. We can join in a global conversation and the electronic tools of blogging, the internet, websites, video clips and all make taking part very easy.

What effect does it have on us? It may – it *should* – cause us to think about what we write and say, think about how we express ourselves and reflect on the writing of others from the point of view of a writer as well as a reader. If we express ourselves in video diaries on You Tube we might reflect on the way our own presentation imitates – or refuses to copy – that of professional announcers and television presenters. It should cause us to present appropriately the content and the style of our message, down to the basic level of accurate spelling if we want to be taken seriously by an adult audience and conventional spoken usage if we want to be widely understood.

This again is something we can teach in school, and has been a staple of media studies courses and drama departments for a long time. The difference now is that the expensive, dedicated, school recording studio is no longer necessary; we can all broadcast via a laptop and a broadband connection.

Contributing to the global information library is now easy using wikis, blogs, personal websites, and other tools and joining the global conversation has never been easier. But how are they managed? How do they fit into information systems?

Wikis, blogs and personal websites

In the words of Wikipedia itself (http://en/wikipedia.org) it is a 'multilingual, web-based, free content encyclopedia project'. Wikipedia is written collaboratively by volunteers from all around the world. With rare exceptions, its articles can be edited by anyone with access to the internet, simply by clicking the 'edit this page' link. The name Wikipedia is a portmanteau of the words wiki (a type of collaborative website) and encyclopedia. Since its creation in 2001, Wikipedia has grown rapidly into one of the largest reference websites.

A wiki allows any of us to participate in writing the world's book of knowledge. With that power comes the need to be responsible, and the recognition that unless and until your contribution is evaluated by others ('peer reviewed' in scientific terms) or overseen by a wise editor, readers must treat it with caution.

Blogs are online diaries and as such are clearly opinions, points of view rather than agreed facts.

Personal websites may seem factual but in fact be heavily biased. Without appearing as blogs and without the checks and balances of peer-reviewed wikis personal web pages are potentially the most misleading information sources of all, especially where their authorship is unclear.

As an avenue for personal expression the Web has given us a global audience. That audience, however, needs to listen with scepticism.

Information systems

An information system can be as complex as that used to deliver passports and driving licences, or to track all the citizens of a large country with massive databases and functionality, or it can be as simple as a club address list where members contact the secretary who in turn updates the list. A large system has security issues, access rights at different administrative levels and intricate functionality in turn linked to other systems, but the thing that turns the database/address list into a formal system is checking, updating and data flow.

For our club, members fill in a form and that arranged and formatted data is then transferred to the database. Whether this is online and electronic or pen and paper makes no difference to the basic system. Members are then urged to inform the secretary of changes in address and phone number and perhaps there is a regular check when subscriptions come up for renewal. It is the regular system of checks leading to updating that makes this an effective system.

Making a system more effective could involve technology or more checks. The club could move from paper forms to a database or spreadsheet and this could bring about advantages such as ease of sharing, efficient checking, reordering and searching.

Organizing the club's annual day out could be done at meetings, by phone or by email, with the advantages of personal contact versus time efficiency and keeping a record of agreements. Greater effectiveness might be achieved via a wiki, in which instead of emails spread around members' mail boxes, a single central collection of agreed comments is available to all, up to date and editable. In a wiki all members can edit and save changes to arrive at a collectively agreed text. Most wikis have the facility to check who made changes and when so you can roll back changes if they prove unsatisfactory.

In the end the choice is open to the users. I may prefer a spreadsheet, you a database and our friend a beaten-up address book. You prefer a PDA and I'll continue with my Filofax. But both of us need an information system to ensure our data is up to date and correct.

The suggestion that all schools report continuously to parents on the progress of their children sounds like a political suggestion rather than an educational one, and one which sends shudders down the spines of teachers and information specialists alike. Requiring continuous assessment and recording, inputting to a centralized safe database which can output to parents on demand from distant terminals while maintaining integrity and security sounds like an expensive disaster in the making. Add to this the inevitable email traffic from dissatisfied parents querying the figures and comments and a damaging spiral is complete. This is just one of many worthy ideas that need detailed management of information if it is to succeed.

Limitless information

Information is a resource which is limitless – and indeed expanding exponentially. Where fossil resources are becoming exhausted and agricultural resources are limited by climate and space, information keeps on growing. Which poses problems in even trying to measure it.

'How much information is there in the world?' is a beguilingly simple question – but the answer is hugely complex. We would have to consider the medium in which it is stored, how to measure how much in terms of weight (books), bulk (film spools) or bytes (computer data). What of the many megabytes used to codify the design of a book against the few used to record plain word-processed text, or a text message, or an email? What of the difference between a picture and writing? Or a high-definition picture from a low-resolution version, an MP3 sound file versus a AVI film clip? And none of this would distinguish between useful and useless value, accurate and inaccurate, duplicated, copied, disinformation or misinformation.

The 'How Much Information' project at the University of Berkeley expresses electronic byte size as follows:

Kilobyte (Kb) 1,000 bytes

2 kilobytes: a typewritten page
100 kilobytes: a low-resolution photograph

Megabyte (Mb) 1,000,000 bytes

1 megabyte: a small novel
4 megabytes: a high-resolution photograph

---

5 megabytes: the complete works of Shakespeare
10 megabytes: a minute of high-fidelity sound
100 megabytes: 1 metre of shelved books
600 megabytes: a CD-ROM

Gigabyte (Gb) 1,000,000,000 bytes

1 gigabyte: a pickup truck filled with books
20 gigabytes: a good collection of the works of Beethoven

Terabyte (Tb) 1,000,000,000,000 bytes

1 terabyte: 50,000 trees made into paper and printed
2 terabytes: an academic research library

Petabyte (Pb) 1,000,000,000,000,000 bytes

2 petabytes: all US academic research libraries
200 petabytes: all printed material

Exabyte (Eb) 1,000,000,000,000,000,000 bytes

2 exabytes: total volume of information generated in 1999
5 exabytes: all words ever spoken by human beings

All of which simply shows there's a lot of it about and gives us highly inexact measures to count it with – though no criteria to measure its worth. Now that you can buy a terabyte hard drive for £100 storage size has become less important.

We can be sure that the amount is expanding, though by how much is hard to express. At the time of writing:

You Tube (which simply didn't exist until recently) streams 100 million video streams a day.

A billion MP3 songs are shared on peer-to-peer sites every day.

London's 200 traffic surveillance cameras send 64 trillion bits a day to the command data centre.

I take this from *The Expanding Digital Universe*, by John F. Gantz, published by IDC in 2007. I have no way of proving or disproving his estimates, despite Ganz explaining his methodology, but as examples of general growth of information rather than precise measures I have no doubt that it is true.

My first computer had 4 Mb of memory and held everything on a single floppy 800Kb disk. There was no hard drive. I'm writing this on a MacBook with 112 Gb of hard drive space and 2Gb of memory. Though I can type slightly faster than I did 20 years ago, my brain is no quicker and my very human memory is no greater. So, while my computer has come on in leaps and bounds I have more stuff to take in but no more brain power to process it with.

The main issue, however, is not how bloated the application is (though it's worth noting that just the paragraph above, saved as a Word document, is 44Kb, while saved as a plain text file it's just 4Kb). The main issue is the quality of the information, how it's stored and retrieved and above all how we each make use of it.

I don't much care whether the answer to my question, 'What's the score?' comes as a text message or in PDF format because the answer will still be England 4 Germany 2. However, 'How was the game?' could be answered with a succinct text message, a quick summary on a blog, a short audio comment via a mobile, a thorough written article with photographs and graphics in a newspaper or a multimedia presentation using streamed video. And, given that choice, I want to choose in an informed way. I may want to select from the information given and I may want to repurpose that information for a variety of audiences, so the form and the content is significant.

Information literacy is important because in a data-rich world we need the skills to separate the useful from the irrelevant and the skills to convert that into useful and usable knowledge. A core of basic knowledge – principles, fundamental rules and essential information which are learned, remembered and understood – will always be necessary, but beyond that it is the skills of information literacy which enable us to grow infinitely. What is important today may be irrelevant tomorrow; old skills take time to unlearn but we must be prepared for change and we need the skills to make that change for ourselves. In a lifetime of learning it should not be necessary always to go back to school and be told. We can be empowered to guide our own learning through supported self-study, online courses and through virtual learning environments.

Document management

A personal document management system has a lot in common with a good filing system. Think of the usual topics and jobs you deal with, label a folder for each one, place them in alphabetical order in the filing cabinet and when you add documents place them in the front of the folder. Now you have an efficient paper filing system in both alphabetical and chronological order.

An electronic filing system is similar: name the folders, place them in there manually or automatically according to pre-set criteria and the operating system will allow you to arrange and rearrange the contents in a variety of ways, according to date created, date modified, size, format, etc. A larger system to be shared by a variety of users will need more organizing and may need a manager or an editor to ensure the system is being adhered to and is consistent. Probably a unique ID number will be given to each file and there will be a place for metadata to be added, giving additional information on who created it, key words for searching by, likely audience, an expiry date, etc. A useful addition would be the facility for users to be emailed when the expiry date is reached and perhaps a means of signing up to receive news of new resources added to the system.

One of the weaknesses of an electronic filing system is the tendency for its users to be inconsistent. In traditional terms this means the filing clerk too easily files the document under the wrong heading and the document seems to be lost. More formally we can say that the metadata is fragile or inconsistent. More forcefully this has been described as 'metacrap'.

Cory Doctorow (2001) who popularized the phrase identified seven obstacles to reliable metadata.

1. People lie
2. People are lazy
3. People are stupid

4.   Mission Impossible: know thyself
5.   Schemas aren't neutral
6.   Metrics influence results
7.   There's more than one way to describe something

So even sacking the filing clerk won't solve the problem.

Content management

Content management is more subtle than document management in that content can appear in smaller chunks and be integrated with other content if required. The content may also be separated from the style of presentation so the final user can choose a style in which to view it. Generally a content management system (CMS) is more flexible than a document management system (DMS). It may track and inform users and editors of changes and will allow greater variety of view by the end user. The content will not be restricted to documents but will incorporate text, graphics, multimedia, webcams, podcasts and interactive features such as updatable weather forecasts, RSS news feeds, shared calendars and online hosted programs. iGoogle www.google.co.uk/ig?hl=en is a popular and user-friendly example of one kind of CMS and Pageflakes www.pageflakes.com/ is another, where the user has limited choice over what is delivered. Wikipedia lists well over 50 free and open-source software CMS systems (e.g. Drupal, Joomla, Mambo, OpenCms, PHPFusion, WordPress, Movable Type), and nearly 30 commercial products, of which perhaps Microsoft Office SharePoint is the best known.

Semantic web

Most advanced of all is the so-called semantic web. This a common framework that allows data to be shared and reused across application, enterprise and community boundaries. Tim Berners-Lee (1999) originally expressed the vision of the semantic web as:

I have a dream for the Web [in which computers] become capable of analyzing all the data on the Web – the content, links, and transactions between people and computers. A 'Semantic Web', which should make this possible, has yet to emerge, but when it does, the day-to-day mechanisms of trade, bureaucracy and our daily lives will be handled by machines talking to machines. The 'intelligent agents' people have touted for ages will finally materialize.

The vision of the semantic web is 'to extend principles of the Web from documents to data'. It allows data to be shared by wider communities, and to be processed automatically by tools, sometimes known as 'intelligent agents'. Tools are available to define logical relationships among resources – 'semantic links' – so users generate files that make relationships between data, allowing machines to follow links and automatically integrate data from many different sources.

Currently the semantic web has only been realized in specialized communities with well-defined resources and needs, but it does seem to be a promising development that could create effective knowledge bases with consistent standards while reducing the need for human interference. Which leaves the hard work to the intelligent agents while intelligent humans apply the knowledge the agents have assembled.

The future of information

There is no doubt that in the short term the quantity of raw data will continue to grow, at an ever-increasing rate. Hard-drive capacities will increase to hold it, operating systems develop to organize it, computer processors speed up to cope with increasingly complex routines, so we won't run out of computer space to store it or computer time to process it. What we also know is that the human brain has not developed at the same rate. Our eyes, brain processes and memories have not kept pace with the blizzard of information.

How useful all this raw data will be is unknown, as it may be

177

duplicated or slightly modified copies of what is already in existence. However new knowledge, new discoveries and new commercial products are sure to produce considerable quantities of new data, as will the continuing desire of the individual and interest groups to promote themselves. In other words the 'blog clog' is set to continue unabated and if the semantic web or an equivalent suite of programs and plug-ins run by intelligent agents can filter, organize and analyse this for us then it may come just in time to prevent us drowning in knowledge.

Nevertheless we cannot use this possibility as an excuse for not learning to use information skills. The old programmer's motto 'GIGO' – put garbage in you'll get garbage out – demonstrates it is even more important that we understand the principles of searching and sorting if a computer is to do it for us, in the same way that basic mathematical skills are essential to check the decimal place on your calculator or estimate the likely change from a purchase in a shop. Meanwhile the global conversation goes on, and you'd be better off taking part in it than just listening from the sidelines.

FURTHER READING

Websites (current at 2008)

These links are available online at www.putlearningfirst.com/findout/

American Library Association – Information Literacy www.ala.org/ala/acrl/acrlissues/acrlinfolit/informationliteracy.htm

Author's Licensing & Collecting Society Ltd
www.alcs.co.uk

Blooms Taxonomy of Learning Skills
www.coun.uvic.ca/learn/program/hndouts/bloom.html

Bogus Research Uncovered
www.work-learning.com/chigraph.htm

Booktrusted
www.booktrusted.com/

Children Decide: Power and Participation in the Classroom
www.cfbt.com/evidenceforeducation/default.aspx?page=316

Comparison of Information Skills Process Models
www.big6.com/showarticle.php?id=87

Credit card fraud
www.consumer.gov p.178

Critical Thinking and Problem-Solving Skills
http://falcon.jmu.edu/~ramseyil/critical.htm

Effective use of PowerPoint in history lessons
www.schoolhistory.co.uk/powerpoint/

Freemind
http://freemind.sourceforge.net/wiki/index.php/Main_Page

Geograph
www.geograph.org.uk

Google Scholar
http://scholar.google.com/

Handling Data at KS3 ICT
http://ngfl.northumberland.gov.uk/keystage3ictstrategy/
KS3Handlingdata.htm

Hyperword
https://addons.mozilla.org/en-US/firefox/addon/1941

ICT Presentations
www.standards.dfes.gov.uk/ schemes2/ secondary_ICT/ ict02/

Local studies research
www.putlearningfirst/brampton/

Mind Tools SWOT analysis
www.mindtools.com/pages/article/newTMC_05.htm

Mind Tools Information Skills
www.mindtools.com/pages/main/newMN_ISS.htm

Open Office
www.openoffice.org/

Plagiarism
www.lemoyne.edu/library/plagiarism/index.htm

Plague Disaster Project
www.putlearningfirst.com/plague/

Plan a Holiday
www.putlearningfirst.com/holiday/

PowerPoint in the Classroom
www.actden.com/pp/

PowerPoint Tutorials
www.internet4classrooms.com/on-line_powerpoint.htm

Presentations
www.standards.dfes.gov.uk/schemes2/secondary_ICT/ict02/
P.116)

Problem-based learning
www.udel.edu/pbl/

Rhetoric, Language in Use
www.putlearningfirst.com/language/20rhet/20rhet.html

School Library Association
www.sla.org.uk

School spending on books
www.booktrust.org.uk/schoolspending/report.htm

Sci-journal
www.sci-journal.org/

Scrivener
www.literatureandlatte.com/scrivener.html

Summarizing
www.bbc.co.uk/skillswise/words/reading/summarising/
factsheet.shtml

Teachers First – Putting Discovery into the Curriculum
www.teachersfirst.com/summer/webquest/quest-a.shtml

The Book Check Assessor
www.books-raise-standards.co.uk/

The Booktrust
www.booktrust.org.uk/

The Forest of Rhetoric
http://humanities.byu.edu/rhetoric/silva.htm

The Microsoft Office Templates for Education
http://office.microsoft.com/en-us/templates/

The Owl Writing Lab
http://owl.english.purdue.edu/

The Radio Days WebQuest
www.thematzats.com/radio/

The School Library and the Key Stage 3 Strategy
www.standards.dfes.gov.uk/keystage3/respub/en_library

Thinking Skills in Primary Schools
www.standards.dfes.gov.uk/thinkingskills/

Visuwords
www.visuwords.com/

WebQuests UK
www.webquestuk.org.uk/

Books and articles

Berger, P. (1998), *Internet for Active Learners*. Chicago, IL: American Library Association.

Berners-Lee, Tim and Fischetti, Mark (1999), *Weaving the Web*. San Francisco, CA: Harper, Chapter 12.

Brown, S. (2006), 'Top 10 most common passwords', www.modernlifeisrubbish.co.uk/article/top-10-most-common-passwords. Accessed 26 May 2006.

Burningham, J. (1978), *Would You Rather*. San Francisco, CA: Chronicle Books.

DfES (2003), *Excellence and Enjoyment – A Strategy for Primary Schools*. London: DfES.

Doctorow, Cory, 26 August 2001, 'Putting the torch to seven straw-men of the meta-utopia', www.well.com/~doctorow/metacrap.htm. Accessed 10 December 2007.

Eisenberg, M. and Berkowitz, R. E. (1990), *Information Problem-solving: The Big Six Skills Approach to Library & Information Skills Instruction*. www.big6.com/index.php. Accessed 17 March 2008.

Eisenberg, M. and Berkowitz, R. E. (1991), *The Big Skills Approach to Library and Information Skills Instruction (Information Management, Policy, & Services)*. Stamford, CT: Ablex Publishing Corp.

Engleberg, Isa N. (1994), *The Principles of Public Presentation*. New York, NY: HarperCollins.

Grey, Duncan (2001), *The Internet in School* 2nd Edition. London: Continuum.

Grey, Duncan (2005), *ICT in English: Adding Challenge, Improving Engagement*. Bristol: Tribal Education/CTAD.

Grey, Duncan (2006a), *Getting The Buggers to Learn*. London: Continuum.

Grey, Duncan (2006b), *Implementing an Information Literacy Programme in Your School*. Bristol: Tribal/SfE.

Henczel, S. (2007). *Information Auditing Report and Tool Kit*. www.fumsi.com/. Accessed 10 December 2007.

Herring, James E. (1996), *Teaching Information Skills in Schools*. London: Library Association Publishing.

Kelly, K. (2006),'From the days of Sumerian clay', *New York Times* 14 May. www.nytimes.com/2006/05/14/magazine/14publishing.html. Accessed 16 November 2007.

LISC Report (1984), *School Libraries: The Foundation of the Curriculum*. London: HMSO.

Lyman, Peter and Varian, Hal R. (2003) *'How Much Information' 2003*. www.sims.berkeley.edu/how-much-info-2003. Accessed 10 December 2007.

Miller, G. A. (1956), 'The magical number seven, plus or minus two: some limits on our capacity for processing information', *Psychological Review*, 63, 81–97.

The Expanding Digital Universe: A Forecast of Worldwide Information Growth Through 2010. http://www.emc.com/about/destination/digital_universe/. Accessed 20 march 2008.

Toffler, A. (1970). *Future Shock*. London: Random House.

Toffler, A. and Toffler, H. (1998). *Rethinking the Future*. London: Nicholas Brealey Publishing Ltd.

US Identity Theft Task Force (2007), *Combating Identity Theft, A Strategic Plan*. www.idtheft.gov/reports/StrategicPlan.pdf. Accessed 10 December 2007.

Winebrenner, S. (2001), *Teaching Gifted Kids in the Regular Classroom*. Minneapolis, MN: Free Spirit Publishing Inc.

APPENDICES

Appendix 1

Information literacy and the National Literacy Strategy

The appendices are available in Word format for classroom use as A4 sheets. Visit www.putlearningfirst.com/findout/

The extracts below are from Reception and Year 1. They show how the NLS target relates to the 20 skills described in Chapter 3 and the Nine Question Steps in Chapter 4.

Reception	Skill	Nine Question Steps
Word level		
Pupils to make collections of personal interest or significant words and words related to particular topics.	- Selecting sources - Sorting and arranging	- Examine, select, reject individual resources - Record and sort information
Text level		
Pupils to locate and read significant parts of the text, e.g. picture captions, name of key characters ...	- Finding information within sources - Reading for meaning	- Interrogate resources

Pupils to think about and discuss what they intend to write, ahead of writing it.	- Making decisions - Evaluating material	- Formulate and analyse need
Pupils to use writing to communicate in a variety of ways ...	- Presenting - Writing clearly	- Present, communicate

Source: www.standards.dfes.gov.uk/primary/

Year 1	Skill	Nine Question Steps
Word level		
Pupils to make collections of personal interest or significant words and words linked to particular topics ... (1 i 12)	- Selecting sources - Sorting and arranging	- Examine, select, reject individual resources - Record and sort information
Text level		
Pupils to make simple lists for planning, reminding ... (1 i 15)	- Note making - Sorting and arranging	- Record and sort information
Pupils to identify and discuss characters, e.g. appearance, behaviour, qualities; to speculate about how they might behave; to discuss how they are described in the text; and to compare characters from different stories or plays. (1 ii 8)	- Finding information within sources - Reading for meaning - Skimming and scanning - Evaluating material - Developing ideas	- Examine, select, reject individual resources
Pupils to build simple profiles of characters	- Developing ideas - Presenting	- Interpret, analyse, synthesise, evaluate

187

from stories read ...
describing ... with
pictures ... captions
... (1 ii 15)

Pupils to predict what a given book may be about from a brief look at both front and back covers, including blurb, title, illustration; to discuss what it might tell in advance of reading and check to see if it does; ... (1 ii 19)	- Selecting sources - Finding information within sources - Reading for meaning	- Examine, select, reject individual resources - Interrogate resources
Pupils to use simple dictionaries, and to understand their alphabetical organisation; ... (1 ii 20)	- Finding information within sources	- Interrogate resources
Pupils to understand the purpose of contents pages an indexes and to begin to locate information by page numbers, and words by initial letter. (1 ii 21)	- Finding information within sources	- Interrogate resources
Pupils to recognise that non-fiction books on similar themes can give different information and present similar information in different ways. (1 iii 17)	- Evaluating material	- Interpret, analyse, synthesise, evaluate
Pupils to identify simple questions and use text	- Questions - Finding information	- Formulate and analyse need

| to find simple answers. Pupils to locate parts of text that give particular information ... (1 iii 19) | within sources | - Interrogate resources |
| Pupils to write own questions prior to reading for information and to record answers, e.g. as lists, a completed chart, extended captions for display, a fact file ... (1 iii 22) | - Questions
- Note making
- Reading for meaning
- Presenting | - Formulate and analyse need
- Record and sort information
- Present, communicate |

Source: www.standards.dfes.gov.uk/thinkingskills/guidance/581458

Clearly, information literacy starts early with fundamental enquiry and communication skills. The skills continue in the Research and Study Skills Strand of the National Literacy Strategy for KS3.

Appendix 2

Questions and decisions 1

'Education is about learning to ask better questions'

Q	Example	Your questions
Who	... did it ... do I ask ... can I compare with ... would be an expert on this ...	
What	... do I do next ... is the question or task ... do I need to find out ...	
Why	... did this happen ... does it say that ...	
Where	... can I find ... do I have to go ... do I go next ...	
When	... can we start ... does this have to done by ... is this available ...	
How	... do I get ... do I use ... do I make ... can I get to ...	

Appendix 3

Questions and decisions 2

'Education is about learning to ask better questions.'

Use this chart to prompt 'Who did ...?', 'What might ...?'

Q	Is ...	Did ...	Can ...	Would ...	Will ...	Might ...
Who						
What						
Why						
Where						
When						
How						

Appendix 4

Define the task

If you are looking at a task rather than directly answering a question, defining that task is essential. We need to know what we have to do, what kind of product is needed before we start. Be systematic, and ask 'What do I have to do?'

Pupil's name . . . . Teacher's name . . . .

```
┌──────────────────────────────────────────────────┐
│  The main task                                     │
│                                                    │
│                                                    │
│                                                    │
│                                                    │
│                                                    │
│                                                    │
└──────────────────────────────────────────────────┘
```

Additional Information   **Your notes**

Topic/general area

Length/duration

Medium

Deadline/Key dates

Restrictions or permissions

Recommended sources

Key words

Appendix 5

Problem solving: the SWOT analysis

All information literacy is a kind of problem solving. It's finding a solution to the problem of too much information, how to sort it out and make use of it. Remember that sometimes the same feature is a strength and a weakness (giraffes see further but have difficulty in hiding. Being single-minded may help solve some tricky problems but is a drawback when making creative solutions).

Pupil's name . . . . Teacher's name . . . .

+ Strengths +	– Weaknesses –

+ Opportunities +	- Threats -

Appendix 6

Identifying sources

Information sources will vary according to the question. Add your local and available sources, with address, phone numbers, Dewey number, web address, email address, etc. Where should I search? Where could I go?

Pupil's name .... Teacher's name ....

People (teachers, family, experts, local politicians)	**Places** (library, internet, public buildings such as careers office, Citizen's Advice Bureau, archives, local records offices)

Information stores (databases, online and CD-ROM encyclopedias, archives, museums, dictionaries, atlases, catalogues)	**Media** (books, websites, databases, television, film/ video, CD-ROM, DVD)

Appendix 7

Selecting sources

Go back to the primary question.

When you select, collect, identify relevant sources, ask 'Which resources shall I use? Does the information I've found help answer that?'

If not, leave it out.

Your teacher will advise you on:

☐ Number of resources you can use at one time (don't hog all the best materials!)

☐ Minimum total of different resources you must use (use a range of materials)

☐ Minimum number of books

☐ Other printed material

☐ Videos/CDs/DVDs/websites

☐ People to ask

☐ Others

Finally you can rate or rank the resources on a 10 point scale (1 is the most useful, 10 the least).

No.	Name	Description	Resource type	Rating
1				
2				
3				
4				
5				
6				
7				
8				
9				

Appendix 8

Evaluating material

Evaluating resources and sources of information requires intelligence and an understanding of the subject, but can be helped by a simple check list. Try weighing arguments, triangulating sources, verifying sources. Examine, select or reject sources in turn.

For each resource fill in the tick chart (see overleaf) then give it a rating between 1 (excellent, reliable) to 10 (almost certainly unreliable).

Resource	Currency			Authority		Accuracy			Objectivity	Usability	Rating 1–10
	Up to date	Well-known publisher or author	Appropriate web address	Author or publisher with high reputation	Recommended by respected sources	Agrees with other sources	No spelling or grammar errors	No known factual errors	No known bias	Is it useful to me?	

Appendix 9

The argument table

This is a useful way of sorting and arranging material. Identify each separate point then think – is it for or against the argument? If you can't decide or if it's not clearly one or the other, add it in the Other box. You'll then have an argument of organized points.

Proposition or argument

For	Against

Other

Appendix 10

Evaluation

The evaluation document for gymnastics, below, is used as a continuing check on progress, creating targets for the next lesson and giving pupils the time to think about what they have done, how they have done it and what they can do next.

GYMNASTICS PROFILE

Name .... Class .... Date ....

Choose a statement which describes you best in this lesson. Write down what you did to earn that statement.

Statement	*How you earned it*
1. I concentrated on the good quality of my movement	
2. I handled the apparatus with care	
3. I experimented with my ideas and movements	

4. I worked hard and tried
   my best

5. I improved some of my
   movements

6. I built an interesting
   sequence of gym
   movements

7. I worked well with other
   people

8. I listened carefully to other
   people

Now choose one of the statements above.

Make it one which did not fit you very well – but which you'd like to work on next time.

Copy the statement into one of the boxes.

Use it as your target for next lesson.

Next time I will try to ...
Next time I will try to ...
Next time I will try to ...

Working with my knees, ankles and toes

Body part	Very good work	Good work	Needs practice
Straight knees			
Straight ankles			
Pointed toes			
Knees, ankles and toes beautifully controlled			

Appendix 11

Which model suits us best?

Model	Pros	Cons
Nine Question Steps		
Big Six		
Five Steps		
GNVQ		
Three Big Steps		
Hinchingbrooke		
Need a Hand		
QUICK		

Our Own Model

Index

7 Ps of presentation 86–8
Art and Design 25, 33
backups 136–7
Big Six 105
brainstorming 64–5
building blocks for library success
    142–7
case studies 99–104
citing sources 93–6
Citizenship 33
comparing sources 16
content management 176
core knowledge 11
cross checking sources 17
curriculum activities 44 ff
    WebQuests 44
    plan a holiday 46
    local studies 46
    plague disaster project 47
    inventions and discoveries 48
    newspaper day 48
    decision making 49
    short fillers 50
    planned designs 50
    problem-based learning 50
    orienteering 51
    museum of pop music 52
cyberbullying 129
data collection 124–5
decisions, making 62–4
defining the task 60–2

Design & Technology 26, 33
developing ideas 82–4
document management 175–6
English 26, 34
evaluating 76–9, 96–7
fact and opinion 21
Five Steps 106
Geography 27, 35
Hinchingbrooke Six Step Plan
    108–9
History 27, 36
identifying sources 67–8
identity theft 131–2
Information advantages 116–17
    audit 123–4
    garbled 135–6
    limitless 172–5
    literacy 2
    poor school 126
    privacy 127–8
    rich school 127
    security 129–30
    strategies 98 ff
    systems 170–2
Information and Communications
    Technology 28, 36
knowledge economy, the 15
known unknowns 11
librarian 115, 117, 142–7
library catalogues 158
library/resources policy 148–51

Index

limiting risk 130–1
literacy 41
locating sources 68–70
Mathematics 29, 38
methodical information strategies
98 ff
Modern Foreign Languages 30, 38
Music 38
Need a Hand model 109–10
Nine Question Steps 105, 112–13
note making 79–80
NVQ model 107
Personal, Social and Health
Education 31, 38
Physical Education 39
plagiarism 133–5
policies 120
policies library/resources 148–51
presentation 84–8
presenting findings 84–8
problem solving 65–6
question, asking the right 5
questioning, teaching the art 5
questions 57–60
Quick model 110
reading for meaning 72
reliability 12
Religious Education 30, 40

resources centre 141–7
rhetoric 90–93
scanning 74–6
Science 30, 40
search engines 153ff
searches, improving 155–8
selecting sources 70–1
semantic web 176–7
serendipity 2
skills, the main 7
skimming 74–6
sorting 81–2
sources
  citing 93–6
  finding information within
    71–2
  identifying 67–8
  locating 68–70
SQ3R 73–4
strategies methodical 98 ff
SWOT analysis 115–16
symptoms of poor information use
  125–6
task, defining the 60–2
Three Big Steps 107
websites 180–2
wikis 170
writing clearly 88–90